7 30 74

MR. & MRS. NORMAN G. SLATE
ROUTE 1 JOY LANE
GREENBRIER, TENNESSEE 37073

Mr. & Mrs. Norman Slate
10724 East 19th Place
Tulsa, OK 74128

BUS THEM IN

BUS THEM IN

BY GARDINER GENTRY

Published by
CHURCH GROWTH PUBLICATIONS
Nashville, Tennessee

BUS THEM IN by Gardiner Gentry

1st Printing, April 1973
2nd Printing, June 1973

Copyright 1973 by Total Evangelistic Concepts, Inc.
Nashville, Tennessee 37209

Printed in the United States of America

WEEPING FOR THE SUFFERING CHILDREN

Precious little children
Scattered throughout this land
What will become of you
If you miss God's salvation plan. . .

Too young to know the dangers
In this wicked world of sin
No one concerned to tell you
Satan waits to draw you in. . .

When I think of how you are suffering
My heart cries out in pain
To reach you with the gospel
So your life won't end in vain. . .

Oh, cruel one, have a burden
And lend a helping hand
So Satan won't take hold of them
And they can reach the promised land.

                    —Alice Jones Gentry

M. J. PARKER

DEDICATION

This book is dedicated to M. J. Parker. Mr. Parker is the Director of Bus Ministry at Highland Park Baptist Church, Chattanooga, Tennessee. I consider him to be the father of effective organized mass bus evangelism.

Mr. Parker brought in over 1,200 people on 10 buses in April, 1948, at Highland Park Baptist Church. The important thing about Mr. Parker, however, is not how many he has brought in on buses, but how many young preachers he has sent out with a knowledge of how to have a good bus ministry.

During an invitation in Highland Park Baptist Church, in a crowd of 3,200 people, Mr. Parker made his way to the pew where my wife and I were standing. He put his arms around our necks, and said, "Young man, I believe God wants you in the bus ministry." I told him I would pray about it. "Don't pray about it," he said, "for you wouldn't know how to pray about this!" Astonished, I replied, "What do you mean, I don't know how to pray about it?" He went on, "You just don't. I'll tell you what you do—you get into the bus ministry, and then pray that God will let you out!"

I started as a bus pastor the next Saturday. God had used that precious 63-year old saint to help me find His will for my life. And it is with great joy that I dedicate this book to "Cousin" M. J. Parker, my earthly father in bus evangelism.

—Gardiner Gentry

GARDINER GENTRY

FOREWORD

This books is written to help those who want help in starting and maintaining an effective program of bus evangelism. The things I have learned by experience over the past 8½ years have taught me how to have a better bus ministry. Although I am not a writer, I hope that by sharing these experiences, I can help others excell in bus evangelism.

Basically there are three things that I count to be very important in this work, and to its effectiveness:

1. A plea to the parent.
2. A program on the bus.
3. A positive prayer life.

This book does not go into great depth on the last two points. These will be dealt with in two separate books to be published later.

You may be asking yourself, "Why another book on bus evangelism?" It's because methods change with time, but never the message that Jesus saves. I hope this book will provide new methods of reaching people for our Lord and Saviour Jesus Christ.

I wish to express my appreciation to the many people who have helped make this book possible.

—Gardiner Gentry

PREFACE
"BUS THEM IN"
By
Reverend Gardiner Gentry

With the increased growing interest in the Bus Ministry across America, several new publications have come to the front, sharing ideas and methods for building a great Bus Ministry, as well as an individual route.

I am delighted that Gardiner Gentry has decided to put his material in printed form. Brother Gentry has proven himself, not only as a Bus Pastor and Bus Director, but also as a great leader of men. M. J. Parker, for many years Directors of the Bus Ministry of Highland Park Baptist Church in Chattanooga, Tennessee, and the father of the Bus Ministry in America, said of Gardiner Gentry, "He's worth 500 people a year."

Brother Gentry has inspired his men to maintain the highest average per bus attendance in America. The ever-increasing number of professions of faith, baptisms and Sunday School attenders, continually reminds all of us here at Beth Haven Baptist Church of the effectiveness of the Bus Ministry in this area.

The methods and approach listed in this book have been tried and proven, and any church that wants action and results will do well to follow the suggestions and recommendations given.

Tom Wallace
Beth Haven Baptist Church
Louisville, Kentucky

TABLE OF CONTENTS

PART IV

ABOUT THE BUSES

PART V

FILL THE BUSES

PART VI

PREPARING FOR THE FIRST SUNDAY

PART VII

SOME PROBLEMS AND OTHER THINGS

PART I
SO YOU WANT TO BEGIN

CHAPTER 1
WHAT TO DO TO BEGIN
A BUS MINISTRY

In the beginning the idea comes that your church should use bus evangelism. What is the first step you should take to begin planting the seeds in the minds of your people? Basically, it is sharing with your people what is happening all over the land as a result of bus evangelism—and do it from the pulpit! Here are some examples of bus evangelism: See Chart "A".

Preach it from the pulpit. Make it clear that we are lagging behind in this ministry. We are letting people around us go to Hell. We are letting Jehovah's Witnesses and Mormons come in and solicit our people, while we let them go to Hell. Tell them that bus evangelism is the easiest and quickest way there is of reaching people. The usual soul-winning and visitation we do is like going fishing with one pole, and one line, one hook and one worm. We go out to catch one fish at a time. But bus evangelism is like taking a large net, dipping it into the stream, and bringing it in full. We need to go out and bring the people in by the net fulls. Bring them in on buses!

Secondly, let the people know that it is a ministry that costs, but that God will supply the need. He will. We could not afford 50 buses here at Beth Haven. There is no way we could afford it. We were struggling to meet our bills. Yet now we own 50 buses! Preach faith—that God will supply the needs, and He will.

The experience of most churches engaged in effective bus evangelism shows that offerings increase from 25% to 100% after starting bus evangelism! People are tired of sitting in buildings with pretty glass and padded pews, where nothing much happens. You let people start coming down the aisles, and start getting

CHART "A"

NAME OF CHURCH	NUMBER OF BUSES	LOCATION	GROWTH THRU BUSES
A rural church near Scottsburg, Tenn.	(not known)	rural	from 30 to 230 in 23 months
A rural church near Hilldale, Tenn.	(not known)	rural	from 70 to 300 in SS, with 500 in worship
Trinity Baptist Des Moines, Iowa		city	from 39 to 313 in one year
Midway Baptist Phoenix, Ariz.	used cars and buses	city	from 52 to 1436 in SS; 1600 in worship in 1 year
First Baptist, Red Oak College Park Ga.	5 buses	small city	from 300 to 500 in 6 months
First Baptist Port Orange, Fla.	3 buses	small city	163 to 362 in 1 month
Forest Hills Baptist Decatur, Ga.	13 buses	metro city	from 250 to 1400 avg in 3 years
First Baptist Center Point, Birmingham, Ala.	began with 5 buses	suburban	from 950 to 1806 in 6 months
Beth Haven Baptist Louisville, Ky.	17 buses	suburban	from 90 riders to 1717 riders in 20 months
First Baptist Hammond, Ind.	rent 11 buses	inner city	began with 281 riders; now baptize 2200 per year
First Baptist Land O' Lakes, Fla.	4 buses	rural	from 85 to 365 in 7 months
Highland Ave. Baptist San Diego, Calif.	7 buses	metro city	from 276 to 912 in 7 months
Park Avenue Baptist Nashville, Tenn.	6 buses	inner city	from 8 riders to 323 riders in 10 months
Woodlawn Baptist Decatur, Ga.	6 buses	suburban	from 25 riders to 260 riders in 13 weeks
First Baptist Houston, Texas	11 buses	inner city	SS tripled in 10 months; had 1400 additions

16

saved, and being baptized, and the people will give! They will know that their money is needed for reaching people!

Then invite someone to your church who is using bus evangelism effectively, to speak to your people on what bus evangelism is doing, who it involves and what to expect. Let him sell your people on bus evangelism. Your people will get excited, and will want to get into bus evangelism right away!

Thirdly, send your people to a church which has an effective bus ministry. Note that it must be to a church that has an *effective* bus ministry. By this I mean they should average at least 50 per bus each Sunday. Your workers will come back with glowing reports of what they have seen. I would say that 99% of all visitors that come to Beth Haven to see our bus ministry in action, visit with our men, and then see the response of Sunday morning, have gone back with a positive report and their churches are now in bus evangelism. Pastor Robert Warner, of First Baptist Church, Ferguson, Missouri, asked me to come to his church to speak on bus evangelism. I met with 25 to 30 men at a men's retreat. We spent the night at a camp back up in the woods where we roasted a big stuffed pig, and had a great time of fellowship. That night, around the campfire, I presented the challenge of church bus evangelism. As I spoke I could see questions in their minds. They looked at me with amazement, as if what I was saying could not possible be true. As I gave the invitation, I asked how many men were willing to get into this. There were very few, but some did. I later invited those same men to come and visit with us at Beth Haven. They did come, 4 or 5 of them. When they left church, they drove as hard as they could to get back to St. Louis that Sunday night, and tell the church what they had heard and seen! They were so excited and enthusiastic about it, their church voted to go into bus evangelism. These men are doing a tremendous job. Recently, on their first anniversary in bus evangelism, they gave the figures of what had happened during the year. In one year they had a total of 7,898 riders on the buses; contacted 9,450 homes; contacted 31,337 persons; and had 79 decisions for Christ!

Yes, the First Baptist Church of Ferguson, Missouri went out and did the job. Now their auditorium is filled. They are one of the leading churches in Missouri. It cost money, but the church has yet to fail in meeting their weekly needs. They have more than surpassed their needs, and are running thousands of dollars ahead of their budget! They now have six bus routes, and God is blessing these great people. They built a new auditorium, and it is now filled. They are using the children's worship services, and they are almost filled. God's hand is upon them. The pastor had a vision, he preached it from the pulpit, he invited an outside speaker, and then he sent his people to another church to see and hear and be trained.

In this way it is not just one man, but a group of men and women who go back and present to your church what they have seen and heard. They get excited about it. They begin to visit areas and subdivisions themselves. They begin to bring the people in. They sacrifice their Saturdays, and give up their Sundays to do this for God, but the first step is to get them excited about it!

Once you get your bus ministry started, schedule a bus conference at your church. Invite other churches to come, hear, see, go back and start bus evangelism in their churches. I believe we need to share what we are doing in reaching souls for Jesus Christ. It is time we quit building fences around our "areas," and limiting our concern for souls. We give hundreds of thousands of dollars to foreign missions each year. And yet, right at our back door, we let people slip through our fingers, and go into a Christless eternity because no one told them how to be saved! There is no way to make it some one else's responsibility, especially when we have the means to reach them, and can show others how to reach them, too!

CHAPTER 2
STEPS TO TAKE IN BEGINNING AN EFFECTIVE CHURCH BUS EVANGELISM MINISTRY

(adapted from a paper by William A. Powell)

1. Much of the success or failure of church bus evangelism is determined by the way it is begun. Very careful planning and taking every appropriate step will help establish a good beginning upon which you can build an effective and major outreach for your church.

2. The pastor MUST take the lead. He should be thoroughly sold on bus evangelism, then discuss it with, and involve, other staff members.

3. Investigate some churches with a successful bus evangelism program—those that average 40 or more riders per bus per week.

4. Read all the available materials on church bus evangelism. The *"Bus Ministry Power Pack"* from CBE SUPPLY, Box 90361, Nashville, Tenn. is an excellent starter set on which to build your bus evangelism library for your workers.

5. Attend one or two of the full two-day bus evangelism clinics. Arrange to be present when the clinic begins, and stay until the conclusion.

6. Obtain and listen to the tapes of other clinics. They will be valuable for the pastor, as well as other key people in the church, and will be excellent for training bus workers.

7. Consider someone to serve as the Bus Director, preferably as a church staff member.

8. In many areas there are pastors and laymen with successful experience who are available to give assistance. Someone should come and speak to your church about bus evangelism.

9. Plan a calendar outlining the steps to take in getting started.

Set yourself a deadline by which time you will be actually involved in bus evangelism.

10. Begin with at least two buses, regardless of how small your church is! If there are more than 300 members, then begin with one additional bus for each additional 300 members.

11. Lead the church to see the advantage of buying *several* "evangelism" buses rather than using all available funds to buy *just one* "trip" bus.

12. Consider the financing of the bus ministry. Most churches will take a special offering to buy the buses. Many people will want to give money to buy buses when they understand how productive they are. Others will give toward painting, renovating, and lettering the buses, buying insurance and things of this nature. Most churches will pay from $1,300 to $3,000 for retired school buses, depending upon age and condition. More than 95% of the churches purchase their own buses. There are many advantages of purchasing, and some real disadvantages to renting. Can you imagine a church renting their pianos each week?

13. The cost of bus evangelism should be in the "Evangelism" section of the church budget. Some churches who claim that evangelism is the #1 reason for their existence still do not have an "evangelism" section in their budget! The amount of $50 per bus per month is usually adequate for operation maintenance and insurance, along with minor repairs.

14. Begin the Graded Church Services at least two months *before* starting your buses. This provides an opportunity for valuable experience for your workers while there is still a relatively small number of children. Then as the buses bring in larger numbers of children, they are more easily assimilated into an already smoothly functioning Graded Church service.

15. It is obvious that considerable effort, funds and preparation are called for in order to successfully launch an aggressive bus evangelism ministry. Most churches that have done so feel that it is probably the best thing they have ever done. This does not involve nearly as much money and effort as does a building program. But the chances of reaching a large number of people for Christ with a good bus evangelism program is much greater than

it is by erecting buildings. The Great Commission emphasizes reaching people—not erecting buildings!

16. In your desire to have everything ready prior to launching the bus evangelism ministry, remember that nothing is perfect. Do all you reasonably can to get ready, *and then go!* Do not delay beyond reason while waiting for everything to fall in place, or everyone to be in favor of it!

17. Pray very sincerely for God's guidance and blessing. Then trust Him to answer your prayer!

CHAPTER 3
SELLING YOUR CHURCH ON BUS EVANGELISM

Do not go ahead of your members so as to leave them behind you. Take the time necessary to bring their vision, enthusiasm and determination close to your own. In some cases. considerable time may be required to sell most of the members, and you may not be able to gain the approval of everyone. Remember that Jesus did not command us to gain the approval of everyone, but He did command us to take the gospel to every creature!

Help your members to understand the need for evangelizing the area. Show them the field that is white unto harvest. Point out any weakness that may exist in the present efforts of evangelizing the area. Show them that bus evangelism is a very effective tool for this work.

Discuss this with the leaders in your church. This includes the deacons, the church council, the Sunday school workers, the WMU, the Brotherhood, and any other key groups. This will erase some false ideas, plant the proper ideas about bus evangelism. Invite persons from other churches with successful experience in bus evangelism to speak to your members and leaders, and to answer whatever questions they may have. Take some of your key leaders to a bus evangelism clinic.

Then, be sure to maintain a positive mental attitude, and optimism about it. Create an enthusiasm and optimism concerning bus evangelism among the members of the church. But always point out that growth and change go hand-in-hand. Always demonstrate your own commitment to church bus evangelism.

Help your members to see that the best solution to drug problems, alcohol problems, crime, juvenile and adult delinquency, etc. is to Christianize the community. Help them see that bus evangelism will mean the difference between Heaven and Hell for many of them. Help them to see that bus evangelism is a good way for members to become involved in reaching people for Christ in an effective way.

CHAPTER 4
RELATIONSHIP OF CHURCH BUS EVANGELISM TO OTHER CHURCH ORGANIZATIONS

An effective bus evangelism program will bring a large number of new people to the church, most of whom will be children. Their presence will be felt most during the Sunday school, and Sunday morning worship hours. In some cases, they are also brought to the Sunday night services, the Wednesday night services, vacation Bible school, revivals, and to other church activities. Bringing these riders to the church activities for a period of time will often open the door, and prepare the way for an effective ministry with others within the family. A great deal of effort and expense is required in enlisting and bringing the riders to the church. Wisdom and stewardship dictate that special efforts be put forth to insure that worthwhile activities are provided for those brought in on the buses. Attention should be devoted in seeing that meaningful worship services are provided, good Bible teaching classes, proper training units during the Church Training hour, and adequate guidance and training provided at other times they are brought in.

Most churches with an active bus evangelism program place emphasis upon the Sunday morning services. This usually results in a large number of unchurched people being brought for Sunday school. Usually this calls for extra-special efforts on the part of the Sunday school workers. New workers must be recruited and trained, new units created, additional literature provided, adjustment of space, arranging for additional space, and a greatly enlarged effort on the part of the teachers and outreach workers of going into the homes of those new people for the proper ministry. Simply providing trained workers, adequate units, and proper space usually consumes a great deal of effort on the part of the Sunday school organization. And then capitalizing on their responsibility and opportunity of proper ministry in the homes of the new people usually loads the Sunday school organization with all the work they can adequately perform. The same heavy responsibilities are added to the workers in the other organizations and activities for which the riders are brought.

Therefore it is necessary for each organization or activity to which these riders are brought to exercise every possible effort to insure that the best provisions are made for them. It is easy to see that the bus workers must maintain close working relationships with the workers in the other organizations. Each organization should have a definite voice in the decision as to how many people are brought in for their activities. This helps to insure that the bus workers do not overload the abilities and facilities of any organization. And since the bus ministry itself requires many workers, the various organizations are asked to encourage their people to assist the bus workers, if they can do so without jeopardizing their own effectiveness. Otherwise it is often necessary for people to be enlisted in bus evangelism who are not involved in these other organizations.

The usual arrangement is for the bus director to serve on the Church Council on a level of relationship with the directors of the other church organizations and activities, except where the bus director is employed by the church in a staff position. A growing trend among churches is the bus director to be employed either on a part-time or full-time basis. In these cases he usually serves directly under the Pastor, or under the Minister of Evangelism. In many churches, the bus director *is* the Minister of Evangelism. Occasionally someone in one of the church organizations will suggest the possibility of the bus director serving under the direction of some person within their organization. However, this is seen as not being normal or practical, in light of the fact that the bus ministry is directly related to the various organizations and activities of the church. Each of these organizations usually have all they can "say grace over" in providing adequately for those brought in and the proper ministry in their homes.

The bus evangelism ministry is not to be considered as a separate or new program or organization of the church. It is simply a method that is very helpful in evangelizing the community. This is the reason that those working in this ministry come under the general direction of the evangelism leader of the church. The time required for proper administration of a growing and aggressive bus evangelism ministry usually requires considerable staff time. This is probably the reason for the growing trend for churches to employ an experienced man to serve on a full-time basis as the Minister of Evangelism, who then gives direction to all facets of evangelism—including the bus outreach ministry.

CHAPTER 5
SOME THINGS TO CONSIDER

Mark 16:15 reveals that Jesus commanded us to take the gospel to every individual. But do you know that:

1. If all the lost people in the world were lined up single file. it would circle the globe 30 times; that it would get 20 miles longer every day; that if you drove down that line at 50 MPH for 10 hours each day, it would require 4 years and 40 days to get to the end; that during that time the line would have grown an additional 30,000 miles?

2. There are more people alive today who have never heard the gospel than the total population of the whole earth when Jesus commanded us to take the gospel to every creature?

3. Approximately 146,000 people will die within the next 24 hours. Most of these will go straight to Hell without ever hearing of Christ—and for many of them, it is through no fault of their own that they did not hear.

4. Approximately 345,000 babies will be born in the next 24 hours. Unless there are some drastic changes in the activities and programs of our churches, and in the lives of our members, most of these 345,000 babies will live, die and go to Hell without ever hearing of Christ.

5. There is a net increase of the non-Christian population of the world of about 138,000 per day. This means that when we go to church next Sunday there will be about 1,000,000 more lost people than there were at the close of last Sunday. And unless there are some quick and drastic changes in our activities, this year will end with about 50 million more lost people than when the year started!

6. At the rate our denomination is now baptizing people, it would take about 320 years to win the lost people of our nation, and about 4,000 years to win all the lost people now alive in the world.

As Billy Graham has said, "Christianity has its back to the wall, and we are losing the human race generation by generation." Dr. Paul James, Executive Secretary of the Baptist State Convention of New York, illustrates this losing battle by placing two cars on an interstate highway in New York—both headed for Los Angeles. One travels 10 MPH, and the other 100 MPH. It is easy to see how rapidly the slower car falls behind. He explains that the 10 MPH car represents the spread of Christianity, and 100 MPH car represents the exploding population increase!

The year 1969 was the climax of the Crusade of the Americas. This was planned to be the greatest evangelistic endeavor ever undertaken by Baptists, or any other group, since the New Testament Pentecost. Yet our denomination reported about the same *decrease* in the total number of baptisms for 1969, as we had been having in recent years!

There are several reasons why we need to consider church bus evangelism:

1. Luke 14:23 says, "Go out into the highways and hedges and compel them to come in, that my house may be filled." This is one Biblical injunction that we have almost ignored completely!

2. There are people who definitely need transportation in order to get to church—especially the older people.

3. It shows that we really care when we offer to come by and pick them up. It gives our church a good way to live for others.

4. Some people will come with you who would not come alone. This makes our invitation to attend church much more meaningful.

5. Some parents will permit their children to attend providing someone picks them up.

6. A good way to reach adults is through their children.

7. After we bring people for awhile, they get in the habit of attending church. Then some will come in their own cars.

8. It is an excellent way to find some good prospects for salvation and for church membership.

9. This will be the means of some people being saved and becoming dedicated Christians.

10. This will be the difference between Heaven or Hell for some people.

11. This is one way to insure that people attend church and are taught the Bible.

12. The Devil will influence most people so much, that some Christian must take the initiative in bringing them to Christ and

His church. Who did God use to influence you to salvation?

13. Any of our members can help in this worthy project: Go with someone else to enlist riders; go with someone else to pick up riders; telephone prospective riders, etc.

14. It is a good way to develop an effective group of our members in another aspect of outreach. Some of our members (present and future) can serve effectively in bus evangelism who may be reluctant to serve in other ways.

15. It will help our church change from a "come" church, to a "go" church; to change from an "organization" and "meeting" church, to a "working" and "serving" church.

16. This helps to insure that all available space in our buildings is used to maximum efficiency.

17. This makes it possible to have a major increase in attendance without having to provide for a lot of additional parking space.

18. Some churches are winning hundreds of people this way.

19. Because of a long-standing proven truth that:

> People do not come to church,
>   They must be brought;
> People do not study the Bible,
>   They must be taught;
> People do not accept Christ,
>   They must be won . . .

20. Because most Christians have not taken seriously the command of Christ to "preach the gospel to every creature."

BASIC PHILOSOPHY FOR BUS EVANGELISM

The basic philosophy behind bus evangelism is of great importance. Effective bus evangelism is built upon the philosophy of church members going after lost people in obedience to the command of Christ. Without this basic philosophy and desire, a bus—or a whole fleet of buses—would be a complete failure so far as winning people to Christ is concerned. Our city bus system is a fairly large operation, but it is based upon an altogether different philosophy. Therefore it has relatively little value to us in our desire to carry out the commission of our Lord.

The following outlines some of the philosophy of a successful bus evangelism program. We begin by stating the negative approach, or the wrong philosophy, and then move on to the positive, and proper philosophy.

I. Bus evangelism *is* NOT based upon an idea that:
   A. There are large numbers of people who want to come to church, but have no transportation;
   B. That the buses are the most important part of bus evangelism;
   C. That bus evangelism is a new and experimental approach.
II. Bus evangelism IS *based* upon the idea that:
   A. There are many people who do have transportation (but who are not attending church), who would attend if we showed enough interest to invite them, and then go by and pick them up.
   B. Most of those without transportation probably would not begin attending if they acquired their own transportation. But many of them would attend if we showed enough interest to invite them, and then go by and pick them up.
   C. The most important part of bus evangelism are our members who care enough not only to invite people to attend, but to actually go by and pick them up.
   D. This idea is as old as the New Testament. Just offhand, I can cite 10 churches that are operating about 300 buses that bring more than 10,000 people every Sunday. That is an average of about 30 buses per church, and 35 persons per bus. One church owns about 120 buses, operates 100 bus routes, and averages 2,800 riders each Sunday. This church has an average Sunday school attendance of 5,000 each week. They have demonstrated that suburbanites in the middle and upper income brackets will respond in the same way as those in the lower income brackets.
   E. Some of our members actually care enough about reaching people to put forth this extra-special effort.
   F. This is one of the fastest and surest ways of having a significant increase in attendance and conversions.
   G. The major emphasis is *not* to spend a lot of money on buses (only a minimum amount should be spent on buses). The major emphasis is to encourage our members to be-

come involved in bringing a large number of unchurched people to church.

This could be part of a turning point for your church in evangelizing your area. Can any member of your church seriously object to other members using their time to go out and bring in unchurched people? We are well aware that successful and significant bus evangelism will involve a great deal of work, sacrifice, money and Christian dedication. It seems that this is close to the heart of what Christianity is all about in winning the world to Christ. Consider the condition of our world, our nation, and our area. Then consider what we Christians, under God, could do and should do. Then get excited and start a one-man crusade!

> "I realize I am only one—but I am one;
> I am not everybody—but I am somebody;
> I cannot do everything—but I can do something;
> And what I can do—I ought to do;
> And what I ought to do—God being my helper,
> I will do!"

CHAPTER 6
PREPARE FOR INCREASED ATTENDANCE

The church that does not prepare for a large increase in attendance at the start of their bus ministry is in for trouble. There will be confusion in the Sunday school and bedlam in the worship services. Suppose your church is averaging 250, but in the next three months that would increase to 600. Where would you put all those people? It takes planning to provide for all the blessings that God sends.

PREPARE THE CHURCH LEADERS

Send Them

A. Send them in advance to a church that has been through the birth pains of a bus ministry. Let them see and hear. Let them get it first hand.

Preaching About It

B. Prepare your congregation by preaching about it. Tell them that the pews will be packed, and the classrooms will be crowded. Train them to expect more noise than usual in the services.

Longer Services

C. The services will last longer because lots of people will be responding to the invitation, and lots more will be baptized. All this takes time, but spiritual people will rejoice in it.

Crowded Areas

D. Hallways and door entrances will be crowded and congested, especially in bad weather. Bathrooms will have waiting lines, and drinking fountains will have waiting lines. Expect these problems and prepare for them in advance.

Literature Orders Doubled

E. Literature orders will double, and it will almost seem as though you never have enough ordered to meet the needs of the students.

Need For More Teachers

F. There will be an immediate need for more teachers, and teachers helpers. Begin teacher training classes immediately, so you will have teachers ready when you need them. Use the Training Union time to train teachers in the art of teaching the various age groups. And begin to do this at the very outset of your bus evangelism program.

Increased Work Load

G. Prepare the church secretary and the Sunday School secretaries for a greatly increased work load. They will have many more telephone calls, records, forms and letters to handle.

Increased Demand Upon Pastor

H. There will be increased demand upon the pastor for his services in the homes and hospitals. He will be called on for more weddings and funerals, and especially for counseling in homes and marriages that are about to break up. But there will also be the greatest opportunity to win souls than ever before. The opportunities to lead people to Christ will be fifty times more than before, as you first win their hearts, and then their souls.

Late Buses

I. Sometimes the buses will come in late and interrupt the Sunday school. You will always try to avoid this, but there will be times it can't be helped. Sometimes a bus will break down. Sometimes the bus pastor will have 20 new riders to pick up, and will consequently run 20 minutes later than usual. It would be nice if he could just leave earlier and make up the difference that way, but the only way that would be possible would be if he could call all the regular riders and be sure they would be ready earlier. The best he can do is make the needed adjustment in the following week.

Church Too Big

J. There will be some members who will want to leave because the church is getting too big. The common saying is, "I like a small church where I know everyone. I don't like a big church." Pastors, take the time to preach to these people. They don't like to see people saved, because the church keeps getting bigger. They will come and complain, "Our church is just getting too big, and I just don't like this, or that. I don't know all these people, and I just don't feel at home here anymore." The only reason they feel out of place is because they haven't fulfilled their place in carrying out the great commission.

Prospect Cards Needed

K. The minister of outreach should be prepared to make a prospect card for every new person who is enrolled in Sunday school, or who fills out a visitors card in the worship service. Each card represents a home. Each child represents a lost Mom or Dad, or an inactive Christian. These people should be visited by the men or ladies of the church within one month of the first contact. But it is best to allow a week or two to go by so the bus pastor can befriend them, and they can get used to him. Give them time to see that you are really interested in them. In other words, "Don't run them off before you get them in!"

Soul-Winning Opportunities

L. The church with an effective bus evangelism program will never lack for prospects to visit and win to Christ. If your church is already an aggressive soul-winning church, this will open many more doors to you. If your church is lagging behind in winning souls, prepare to have a soul-winning clinic to teach your people how to win the great numbers of people that will be coming because of bus evangelism.

Baptisimal Committee

M. Prepare your baptisimal committee to have adequate places, and clothing for those who come for baptism. We provide everything for the candidates. They do not have to bring anything with them. The converts will need instruction on how to stand in the water, how to remain stiff, how not to look at the congregation, etc. They will also need instruction on what baptism means.

In 1971 Beth Haven baptized 909 converts! So you can see you need to prepare in this area.

Parking Lot Shortage

N. Prepare for a parking lot shortage. If you have 6 church buses, each of them 10 feet wide and 30 feet long, it takes a lot of space to park them. Remember, you have to leave room enough for the riders to get on and off easily, so the buses can't just be jammed in close to each other. You may find that the buses take up a good amount of your present parking area. Work out in advance your traffic patterns as to where the riders will be let off, where the buses will park and where the riders will get on the buses again. This will be especially important in rainy weather. Also check to see if the bus riders will have to cross motor traffic lanes in the parking lot in order to get into the buildings. Always remind your people to be extra careful when driving in the church parking lot, because a four or five year old cannot be seen over the hood of a big car. It may be that you can train your deacons and teachers to take the smaller children out to the buses first, and get them on the right bus. Safety is a primary consideration, and you need to prepare yourself and your people for it.

Preparing the Ushers

O. The last thing in preparing your church for a greatly increased attendance is to prepare the ushers. The ushers need to be prepared to handle anything that comes up during the services. A disturbance during the church service can kill the whole spirit of the service. But if the ushers are alert, and have been properly trained, they can handle the situation quickly and quietly, and hardly anyone will know what has happened. For instance, when a baby starts to cry, everyone begins to wish the mother would take the child out. Then they wonder why the ushers don't do something. Then they wish somebody would do something about that crying baby! Well, the ushers should be assigned to a certain section of pews. Any disturbance, any activity or anything out of the ordinary going on in those pews is his responsibility. He should take care of it immediately. The usher should have a couple of lollypops in his pocket in case a child cries. But if he is really alert, he will greet that mother at the door, and direct her to the nursery, all the while assuring her of the quality of care and facilities provided for the little ones. If the mother insists on keeping the child with her in the services, there is nothing to do but to keep alert, and keep some lollypops handy.

If an older child is causing some disturbance, the usher should go to the end of that pew, point to that child and give him the quiet sign. If the usher has to go back the second time, he should motion for the offending child to follow him out of the pew. Then the usher can lead the child to the vestibule of the church where he can sit for the remainder of the service. Or the usher can take such a child and seat him between two adults. The children will soon learn that they must behave, or they will be taken out and made to sit between two adult strangers. The ushers may want to ask the bus pastor, or the bus pastor's wife to sit next to a known unruly child. It is also important for the pastor to remind everyone that they are not to get up during the service. They are not to go for a drink of water or anything else. One day two teenage girls got up and started toward the rear of the auditorium during the service. They made it about half-way when the pastor stopped in the middle of his sermon, and said, "Young ladies, you come right back and sit down in your seats." They kept right on going. He said again, "Young ladies, I said to stop where you are and return to your seats!" They were too embarrassed to go any further. They returned to their seats, and the service continued without further interruptions. Our teenagers know they are not to get up and go out, or the pastor will call them down. And if a younger one goes for a drink of water, he has to go to the bathroom five minutes later, so we don't allow it. So when you see large numbers of people coming into your church, train them from the beginning that they are to remain in their seats until the service is dismissed.

CHAPTER 7
PREPARING YOUR DEACONS

The deacons need some special training and preparation when large numbers of people begin to come on the buses. They especially need training in serving the Lord's Supper. Many of the children have never been in a service where communion has been served, and will not know what to do. Here are some suggestions:

1. The deacons should be sure that all children are seated in pews with plenty of adults between them. If you have pews filled with children, you can expect to have trouble getting the trays of bread and wine through the aisle.

2. Be sure you have enough communion cups and bread trays to care for the increased number of people.

3. The pastor will have to explain each time about the meaning of the Lord's Supper, and who should take it.

4. The deacons will have to be prepared for someone dropping a bread tray, or a tray of communion cups. They will have to know how to handle a child who wants to take a whole handful from the bread tray. They will have to know how to keep calm and make the best of some very awkward situations.

5. If you have a rheostat on your church lighting system you will find it helpful to dim the lights while the communion is being served. This one thing produces a stillness and quietness as does nothing else. It has a great psychological effect on the children.

There is no way to prepare for everything that might happen. But these are some of the most common things to watch for. Your church members can help greatly if they will observe the children and sit themselves where they can be of help in case it is necessary. Try to anticipate every possible problem, and train the deacons in what to do in each case.

PART II
PREPARE TO BEGIN

CHAPTER 8
FIFTEEN PREFERRED PROCEDURES

1. Make sure an adequate number of bus workers are enlisted, trained and dedicated so there will be a good team for each bus route. Each Saturday is used for enlisting riders.

2. Each bus route will need a team. This consists of a driver, who makes sure the bus is clean, fueled, properly maintained, and ready to leave on schedule. It also includes the captain, whose job is to be in charge of everything related to his bus route, and to make sure the bus is filled with people when it returns to the church Sunday morning. Co-captains give general assistance to the captain, and in many cases will be serving an apprenticeship for the time when they become captains. One or more teenagers on each bus assist with the children in such matters as discipline, singing on the bus, personal comfort and safety and things of this nature.

3. Some members who are not heavily involved in other church work can excell in church bus evangelism. Mark Hudson had been a Christian less than six months when he became a bus captain. During his first 20 weeks he averaged 58 riders per week. There were 37 conversions from his bus route during these 20 weeks, and 28 of them were baptized into the membership of the Woodlawn Baptist Church. One of these, a 36-year old man, became a bus driver.

4. It is necessary for some church members to rearrange some priorities, and to change their normal Saturday and Sunday schedules.

5. It is necessary to rearrange some priorities in church activities. Most churches are already heavily loaded with programs and

activities. This cannot be added on as another program on the hope of a surplus of workers and finances.

6. It is best to begin by buying some evangelism buses, rather than one trip bus. Usually it is possible to get three or four retired school buses to use for evangelism for the same price that one good trip bus would cost to use in occasionally transporting church groups for special functions.

7. It is best to purchase the largest buses possible—at least 54-passenger capacity. As a rule the size of these used buses has nothing to do with the purchase price, the insurance cost, the maintenance cost or the operating cost. And it is just about as easy to have an average of 50 riders on a 60-passenger bus, as it is to have 28 riders on a 30-passenger bus.

8. It is best to begin with two or more buses. Any church that cannot generate enough interest to start with two or more buses probably will not have very much success in church bus evangelism. Remember, the attitude of the leaders is the major determining factor in evangelizing the community.

9. It is best to establish the first bus routes near the church building. After an adequate number of routes are established in the local community, then routes can be established in neighboring areas that have large numbers of unchurched people.

10. The procedures used to enlist riders will contribute much toward the success or failure of church bus evangelism.

11. Plans should be made for an increase in attendance of 40 persons for each bus route established. Proper procedures usually result in an average of more than 40 riders within the first two months after a route is begun.

12. The church leaders must plan ahead for a large influx of people in such matters as providing space, rearranging classroom space, and departmental assemblies, to adjust for overcrowded conditions in some classes and departments. You will need to recruit and train new workers, recruit and train members for the important job of counseling children who respond to the gospel, recruit and train members who will go into the homes to win the parents to Christ, and recruit and train members to conduct worship services for the children.

13. Make adequate plans to get off with the best possible start. It may be better not to begin at all, than to begin wrong.

14. Pray for God's guidance and blessings, and trust Him to answer your prayers.

15. Pray as if everything depended upon God. Work as if everything depended upon you.

CHAPTER 9
SIXTEEN FOUNDATION PRINCIPLES

1. Productivity is more significant than creativity or innovation. There is a great need for something productive—not just creative or innovative.

2. Almost unbelievable results are achieved very quickly with church bus evangelism. For example, consider the Zion Baptist Church, Aurora, Illinois. They purchased 3 buses for about $1,600, and started them the first Sunday in March. They had 33 riders the first Sunday, 105 riders the second Sunday, 141 the third, and 176 riders the fourth Sunday in March. This gives them an average of 114 riders each Sunday during the first month. Their Sunday school attendance the last Sunday in February was 243, and this was an all-time high for them. The attendance the first Sunday in March was 251; then 336 the second Sunday; 375 the third Sunday; and 435 the last Sunday in March. This gave them an average attendance of 350 per week in March, and 401 in April compared with a previous high attendance average of 195 in February. Their Sunday school enrollment more than doubled from 198 at the first of March, to 426 at the end of March. They had 12 professions of faith, and 8 by letter during March. During April, 13 more riders made professions of faith.

3. The workers are far more important than the buses. Buses can actually be a liability unless there are dedicated and trained workers available. The availability and dependability of workers is more important than natural ability or personal status.

4. A tremendous amount of work is required. Most successful bus workers devote many hours every Saturday to this work. It also means getting to the church an hour or two early each Sunday morning, and returning home late for lunch. Carlton Goodman averages more than 15 hours per week enlisting riders. Last year he averaged 125 riders per Sunday on his bus route. He has brought in more than 200 riders on four occasions; with a record 244 on one Sunday morning on a three-bus caravan! Each year

there are probably more than 300 conversions as a result of the 1,000 new riders the buses bring to Beth Haven. But this requires more than twenty hours work each Saturday and Sunday.

5. The church members who use every Saturday and Sunday in evangelizing the area will earn some very significant rewards in this life, as well as in Heaven.

6. Most of the riders are children, although adults ride the buses, too. But an understanding of the amount of time and concern that Jesus had for children will cause church leaders to readjust some philosophies and thinking and activities.

7. Most parents want their children to receive religious training. Many do not want it badly enough to get up and take them to church, but they will let the children ride the church bus.

8. An excellent way to reach parents is through their children, even though not all parents will be reached this way. There is great value in having in the unchurched home a child that shares his enjoyable and profitable experience at church. The children riding the bus can help to open the door into the hearts of the parents.

9. One of the best ways to win the world is to win the youth.

10. Most people will not come to church, they must be brought. Most people will not study the Bible, they must be taught. Most people will not accept Christ, they must be won.

11. Jesus never commanded the lost to come to the church, but He did command the church to go to the lost.

12. There will be a large number of problems to face. This includes such things as: providing additional space; recruiting and training additional teachers and workers; finding and purchasing used buses; renovating, painting and maintaining buses; recruiting and training bus workers; handling criticism that may arise; providing adequately for a large number of unchurched children during the worship service; enlisting and training members in counseling with children who respond to the gospel; winning the parents of the children; and maintaining the proper attitude throughout the church.

13. The Devil begins working in every way possible when the church really gets serious about evangelizing the area.

14. God will, and does, greatly bless a church that dares to

change from an average 20th century congregation to an aggressive New Testament church.

15. The blessing of God, and the results accomplished make it worth the cost, the problems and the work.

16. This will give a new direction to the average church. It can help in the transition from a "come meet" church to a "go bring" church.

CHAPTER 10
THINGS THAT CONTRIBUTE TO FAILURE

1. Buying a bus, enlisting a driver, announcing the bus stop schedule, and expecting people to get on just because you now have a bus.

2. Waiting for everyone in the church to favor starting the bus evangelism program. Just one or two key people can delay or prevent your getting started, and lost people will continue to die without Christ;

3. The attitude that bus evangelism will not work for you. That your situation is too "different" or "unusual."

4. A limited vision of the needs and possibilities of bus evangelism in your area. Don't think too small. Matthew 9:36-38.

5. Lack of faith in God and in His ability to use you and your church.

6. Being satisfied with "business-as-usual" procedures, and status quo operations.

7. Failure to see the fields white unto harvest, and that Christ in you is the hope of glory.

8. Doubting the proven truth that the number of people attending your church, and the number being baptized is determined by the attitude and commitment of the pastor and key leaders.

9. A lack of personal commitment that results in the reordering of priorities, schedules, programs and emphasis.

10. Getting off to a poor start in a haphazard way.

11. Failure to recruit a good team of workers for each bus— a captain, co-captain, driver and several teens.

12. Inadequate training for the bus workers.

13. Inadequate organization. Placing the Bus Director under the supervision of a committee, class or organization will result in less efficiency, and hinder the work. Provide a good organization within the bus workers so each can relate to the other

properly in the operation, maintenance, etc. of all the buses.

14. Starting with too few buses. Every church should begin with at least two buses, regardless of how small the church or mission is.

15. Buying an expensive bus as the first bus rather than several evangelism buses.

16. Buying small buses. The buses should be the largest possible—at least 54-passengers capacity. Do not waste money by purchasing the van-type vehicle!

17. The idea that the buses are means of transportation, rather than means of evangelism.

18. Depending upon advertising in newspapers, radio, television or leaflets to cause people to ride the buses.

19. Using the wrong methods to enlist riders.

20. An improper concept of the importance Jesus placed upon children, and His attitude toward them.

21. Failure to provide workers and materials for Children's Church services.

22. The use of improper methods of evangelizing children, and failure to train counselors to deal with spiritual matters with children.

23. Failure to train members in winning the parents.

24. Failure of the bus captain and his team to spend an adequate amount of time every Sunday in visiting and enlisting new riders.

25. A wrong concept concerning special high-attendance Sundays, as to the value of them, how to plan them, and how to promote them for maximum benefit.

26. A wrong concept about the use of contests, gifts, awards and prizes.

27. Failure to provide good programs on the buses enroute to and from the church.

28. Selective evangelism. Passing by certain homes, and skipping certain people, because "that kind" are not welcome at the church.

29. Beginning the routes too far from the church.

30. Failure to prepare your church for a great influx of unchurched people—mostly children.

31. Failure to provide adequate Sunday school space. An unwillingness to relocate classes and departments in order to best utilize the space available will defeat the purpose of bus evangelism. An unwillingness to have two Sunday schools will contribute to failure. An unwillingness to rent adjacent space in homes, store-fronts, or schools will limit your effectiveness in reaching people for Christ.

32. Failure to provide an adequate number of Sunday school teachers and workers.

33. Failure to prepare for, to expect, and to pray for divine wisdom and strength for the enlarged attacks of the Devil upon the church and its members.

CHAPTER 11
16 THINGS THAT WILL KILL A BUS ROUTE

LAZINESS

Laziness will kill a bus route. A man who will not visit on his bus route because he is lazy will kill that route. There is a difference between being lazy and being tired. The man who works two jobs will come home tired. But the man who works just one job, then comes home and props his feet up, has Mom bring him his coffee and has Junior adjust the picture of the T.V.—well, that man is just lazy! When a man gets too lazy to visit his bus route, his bus route will soon die.

LACK OF TRAINING

The man selected for a bus pastor should be a man of great zeal and high prominence. He may even be a deacon, but if he does not have the proper training, he will fail on his bus route. Because he does not know how to go about it, he will soon become discouraged and quit. You would not take a man off the streets, and place him immediately in the front-line of battle. He would not know how to respond to the attacks of the enemy, and gain the victory. The same is true of a bus pastor. If you do not train the man properly, do not expect him to do a good job. If you train him properly, he will build a bus route and keep it going.

LACK OF CONCERN

A bus pastor that it not really concerned about people will not suceed on a bus route. He may be well-trained, and know how to enlist riders. But if he does not have a genuine concern for people, he will fail. I once had a bus pastor who could get 75 or 80 on his bus. But after he picked up the last rider and closed the door, he really couldn't care less about the people. He was very happy that his bus was filled, but he was not personally concerned about the individuals. It soon became apparent, and his route began to go down. It went from over 100 to into the teens. That bus route died because the bus pastor did not have a personal concern for people.

INCONSISTENCY

Consistent visiting every Saturday is a must for a sucessful route. You can't go out one Sunday, and then skip a Saturday. When the World Series is on, you can't decide to skip a Saturday, and try to "go doubly hard" the next week. Do you remember when you were first in love? When a man is in love, he wants to see his girl every night. But suppose one Friday he did not show up. And then on Sunday he did not appear to take her to church. Suppose the same thing happened for several weeks? It wouldn't be long before that girl will think he has found someone he likes better than her! Those who ride the buses think the same way. When the bus pastor sometimes visits, and then sometimes doesn't, they begin to think he must like something else more than he likes them. And before you know it, that bus route has gone down. Inconsistency will kill a bus route.

GROUCHINESS

That's not a hard word to define, is it? Now it may be that on Saturday morning you expect your wife to have all your clothes laid out, ham and eggs cooking and everything ready for you. But one Saturday she doesn't do all those things for you. And that makes you mad. You tell her to get up and lay out your clothes, and get your breakfast. She replies, "You know how to shake a cereal box as well as I do, the sugar's over the stove and the mik is in the refrigerator. Get it yourself! I'm going back to sleep!" Well, you get up and manage to get to the church for the bus meeting. That morning the Bus Director's talk centers around getting you to love people more. He begins to skin your hide because you haven't been loving your people as you ought, and you haven't been as faithful as you could. Then it's time to get out on that route. No one answers your knock at the first door. At the second door, they tell you they can't ride the bus because they're all going to the country for the weekend. At the third door, they make some half-hearted excuse for not coming on your bus. And that about does it! You start to talk mean and hateful. There's a harshness in your words. You become sarcastic, and the people on your route realize that you are a grouch, and they will not come. Grouchiness will kill a bus route.

WORLDLINESS

What does worldliness mean? It means being improperly dressed. The young lady who goes out to visit on the route wearing a mini-skirt may not think there is anything wrong with that. But the mother in the home she visits was brought up in a different time, when short skirts were considered to be very immodest. That mother may not want her children to attend a church where mini-skirts are acceptable. The same is true for a young man with long hair visiting on a bus route. The parent may see the young man as a "hippie," and refuse to allow the children to come. I was brought up in the Elvis Presley era. I wore my hair long with the ducktail in back. I wore my shirts with the collar turned up, trousers low on the hips, and pant legs tight at the bottom. I thought I was with the "on" generation at that time, but I well remember how my parents had a distaste for the way I dressed and looked. It's the same way today. It's best to go out dressed your best as you represent your church to the people on your bus route. I believe that a man's hair ought to be short enough to at least see his ears. And it ought to be short enough to not cover his collar. You may have a different opinion, but I believe worldliness will kill a bus route, because I have seen it happen.

FEAR

If a man is afraid of people, afraid to meet new people, afraid to talk to people, then his bus route will die. I had a bus pastor who was about 6'2", and weighed well over 200 pounds. He came to me one day and said, "Brother Gentry, I'm going to quit. I just can't seem to talk to people. I just don't know how to say the right things. I'm just afraid to talk to people." I said, "Come on, let's go visit together." We went out and began knocking on doors, and it wasn't long before that bus pastor got the victory. He began to open up and talk to people. He began to get people involved, and his route began to grow. He uses one of our largest buses, and consistently runs 70 or more every week. He is doing a fantastic job, but he almost quit because he was afraid of talking to people.

NO PROGRAM ON THE BUS

If there are no songs, no Bible quizzes, no stories, no prayer time, no invitation on the bus, the bus route will go down. There is a chapter devoted to programs on the bus because it is one of the most important parts of bus evangelism. In my opinion, the three most important things in bus evangelism are: 1. A plea to the parent; 2. A program on the bus; 3. A prayer life. The program on the bus brings them back every week. We keep them excited by giving them a preview of the story for next week, of special events coming up, of contests and other promotional ideas. You must have some kind of program on the bus if you expect the riders to continue to come. If the riders just sit there looking out the windows, their minds will be wandering, and some will be a little afraid because of not knowing what to expect on the bus and at the church. Instead of allowing their minds to wander, provide something constructive relating to the Bible to keep their attention.

NO LOVE

You know there is a difference between love and lust. There is also a difference between love and no love, and people can tell if you really love them or not. There was a young man who fell in love with a beautiful girl, but he was separated from her. So he bought 365 post cards, and each day he wrote to her telling of his love for her. One year later the girl was married. But she did not marry the young man—she married the mail carrier! He was the one who came to her door every day spoke to her, and developed the loving relationship that resulted in marriage. You know we must love people, but that love must be expressed on the bus route. If you don't love your people, they will soon find it out. And someone else will come along and love them, and win them and your route will go down. A lack of love will kill a bus route.

NO PRAYER

A failure to pray will kill a bus route. After our bus pastors have visited all day Saturday, they return to the church on Saturday night for a time of prayer and praise for what God has done during the day. We may have a time of confession, and getting right with God. There may be prayer requests for things needed in our bus ministry, or for people on the route, or for our pastor. We meet to pray every Saturday night, sometimes into the early hours of the morning. We have prayer meetings in the church every night of the week. As many as 60 men come to pray and ask God's blessing on our church. We ask God to send us blessing-makers, and keep out the trouble-makers. We have had as many as 80 or 90 saved on Sunday, and I believe it is the result of the visiting and the prayer of our workers. Bus pastors who will not pray, will not succeed on their route, because prayerlessness will kill a bus route.

QUITTING

A quitter is a person who is constantly threatening to quit. He is one who is always discouraged, and convinced that "he just can't do it." He is a hang-dog, droopy person who is always thinking of why he can't succeed, instead of figuring out ways to succeed. A person like this is not going to quit—he has already quit! A quitter will spell doom for a bus route. The unemployment lines are filled with quitters. The welfare rolls are filled with quitters. Quitters always blame someone else for their failure. He always has some excuse for not doing his job right. And rather than get stragihtened out, he would rather quit. A bus pastor who quits easily will be a failure, and kill that bus route.

NO ZEAL

A person who always mopes around, drags himself in like he was half-dead, or who just always seems to be pooped out will never get the job done. Misery loves company. One listless, droopy, dragging man will make others the same way. Learn to go with enthusiasm and with a smile on your face. It is said of one of our bus pastors that he literally abandons his car when he reaches his area. He bounds up to the door, knocks, spends a short time at each house and then goes briskly to the next door. He has zeal and enthusiasm, and he averages over 100 per Sunday on his bus. Lots of zeal will build a route. A lack of zeal will kill a bus route.

WRONG APPROACH

You can begin to brag about your church, your pastor, your buildings, and so many other things. But that's the wrong approach. If you depend on circulars, radio or TV advertising or ads in newspapers, you will not have a successful bus ministry. You must make an appeal to the parent for the children to come tomorrow on the bus. "I need your help, Mrs. Smith. Would you please have the children ready? You won't let me down, will you?" Then leave with a smile, and tell Mrs. Smith how happy you are that she is helping you, and you'll be looking for the children tomorrow morning. Use the right approach. The wrong approach will kill a bus route.

STAYING TOO LONG

Staying too long in the home of a rider will kill your route, because it will keep you from visiting the other homes, and enlisting other riders. One lady called our church and said, "Mr. Gentry, as much as we think of him, your bus pastor is spending too much time in my home. The neighbors may get the wrong idea, and I wish you'd help in this matter." That bus pastor had been spending anywhere from 30 minutes to one hour in that home! That told me he was not enlisting new riders, and his route would fall off. If he had 50 homes on his bus route, and he stayed a half hour in each one, it would take a full day for him to get around his route! It's best to just knock on the door, and enlist the riders as quickly as possible. It is not necessary, and may be embarrassing for you to discuss their utility bills, or doctor bills. If you become a nuisance, they will not let the children come, and your route will die.

FALSE PROMISES

When you promise something make it good! If you promise to give a New Testament on the third Sunday a rider comes, be sure you have the New Testament on that third Sunday! A broken promise to a child will cause that child to lose confidence in you, and will influence his attitude toward the church. So always be sure to keep a promise. Broken promises will kill a bus route.

UNPREPARED TEACHERS

An unprepared Sunday school teacher can kill a bus route. A Sunday school teacher who does not prepare a lesson until Saturday night or even Sunday morning will kill a bus route. Unprepared teachers cannot teach interesting lessons. And riders will not continue to come for lessons that are uninteresting and meaningless to them. The whole purpose of bringing the riders is for them to hear the Word as it is taught in the Sunday school. If the Sunday school teacher is unprepared he defeats the very reason we bring people on the buses! Teachers who do not prepare lessons usually do not visit the members of their class. And between these two-failure to prepare, and failure to visit-the bus route will die.

CHAPTER 12
SELECTING THE BUS ROUTES

There are sevearl kinds of places that are good for bus routes. Before starting out, check all the neighborhoods around the church. Then check on the areas of the city to find out the best places for new bus routes. Starting a route in the wrong place creates a great many problems later on, so start in a good place.

NEW SUBDIVISIONS

A new subdivision is an ideal place, perhaps one of the best there is. Why? Because new people are living there. They may have moved in from out-of-town, or simply from the other side of town, but they have generally lost the association with their former church, if they had one. There are a lot of new subdivisions featuring low-down-payment mortgages. These homes are usually fairly small, but they often have large families living in them. And these neighborhoods will have lots of kids.

GOVERNMENT HOUSING PROJECTS

A second place that is very good is a government housing project. Of course, these will be lower income homes, with all the problems of the poor. In many of these homes there will be no father. Many of the mothers will be divorcees living with their children. But there will always be a lot of people. That does make visitation easier, because you can park your car and walk the whole project. There will always be people out, summer or winter, and it's easy to make contact with them. These are needy people, even when the physcial needs are being cared for. A wife whose husband has left her; children that have no father to correct them. These children become teens, and the mothers have no control over them. If you can get them into the church, under the sound and influence of the gospel, and even active in church work, you will begin to see these same children live changed lives for God.

But you better prepare for competition. Even if no one else

53

is running buses in a project now, they will begin to do so if
you begin to bring a lot of people to your church from there.
A government housing project, about 8 miles from our church,
has no less that 8 buses running in it on Sunday morning! Even
though there are 7 other churches there, our bus usually brings
about 70 people, while the others come out with about 10 or
15 on each. The difference is in the manner of contacting the
people—showing them that you are genuinely concerned about
their welfare, spiritual and physical. Sometimes you will have
to help them get medical attention, or legal aid, or intervene on
their behalf with the court.

APARTMENT COMPLEXES

Another good place is the apartment complexes that are
going up all over our land. The boom used to be in new homes,
but now it's in apartment houses. Almost all apartment houses
will have the elderly as tenants, and some are designed
especially for them. Many of these folks have lost the fulness
and meaning for life they once had. They can no longer care
for a yard and a house, so they live where they have no upkeep
or maintenance at all. But they are often lonely and sometimes
disillusioned with themselves. They need someone to take an
interest in them, and most of them need someone to tell them
about Jesus.

The young married also flock to these apartments. Most young
couples do not have enough money to buy a house when they
get married, so they look for an apartment to rent. These are
ideal places for your soul-winning visitation. There are plenty
of prospects for your WIN school witnessing. Many of these
young marrieds will not ride the bus, but they are prime raw
material on which to build the future of your church. Don't
overlook them just because they do not ride the bus. Jerry
Morrow has a young-married couples class in our church. He
goes out primarily to win young marrieds to the Lord, and has
built his class from zero to 25 couples in just a year-and-a-half!
Now some of these young marrieds are becoming active in the
bus work, and are expanding the ministry.

The apartment complexes will also have the more usual kind
of family unit—mother and father with several children. The

easiest way to detect these kinds of families is to drive through
the area looking for bicycles, kiddie pools, children's clothing
hanging on drying lines, or children playing in the street, or
yard. You may encounter opposition from the apartment manager because he is of a different denomination, or a different
faith, or he may simply be an unbeliever. He may not be in
sympathy with you at all. So find out who *owns* the apartments
when you start out. Go to the owner and sell him on the idea
that you are going to provide a really valuable service for him.
A service that will really benefit him, and not cost him anything
at all. You might say something like this: "Sir, I have been
noticing your apartments over on Horn Street, and it seems
they are beginning to deteriorate much sooner than they should.
It seems the children are breaking up things, and painting on
the walls. It's an odd thing, but a lot of that happens on Sunday
morning, because Mom and Dad have been out on Saturday
night, and gotten themselves all looped up. Or they're just too
tired to get up on Sunday morning, so the kids get up and run
wild by themselves all through the apartments. They just do as
they please, and they are ruining your apartments. Now what
I propose is to get those kids out of the complex on Sunday
mornings, and into church where we can teach them better. We
want to teach them to be better morally as well as spiritually,
and that will help them not to destroy your place. We will
actually provide a baby-sitting service on Sunday morning
while Mom and Dad sleep.

"Now if you, or your apartment manager, will give me the
names and addresses of every new person who moves in, we
will go immediately to that family, and tell them that there is
free marriage counseling, as well as the Sunday morning help.
At the same time we try to get them into church, too. There are
so many parents these days who do nothing but fight and
quarrel, and end up by smashing the furniture, that we know
we can help them before they do such damage. If we can talk
to these people, and let them know we care about them, it may
save your apartment a lot of abuse, and help them be happier.
It will help the neighborhood look better, too. But most of all,
it will help them to live as humans ought to live, and it will
save you a lot of money in the process!"

Now, what can that man say, except "Yes!" So then go back
to the apartment complex, and see the manager. Tell him you
are going to run your bus in there. He may object, but when
he does, simply tell him that you have already seen the owner,
and he has said you are to run your bus there, and help the
people all you can. Also, tell him the owner has given instructions for him to give you the names of all new tenants as soon
as possible after they move in. The manager cannot go against
the owner, so you are in. But be tactful to the manager, because
you want to retain his cooperation and friendship. Try to have
him on your side so he will not complain to the owner at a
later time.

TRAILER PARKS

Trailer parks are also an excellent place to start a bus route.
Many trailer parks have a lot of transient people, but God loves
them as much as anyone else. Again, it's good to go to the
owner and explain what you are doing, and get his permission
to go in and visit. I have been refused only once, and that was
by a Catholic owner who did not want me in his trailer park.
But I had a good Protestant riding my bus who lived next to
the trailer park, and he rounded up the riders, and had them
waiting at his house on Sunday morning. Sometimes as many
as 25 came from that trailer park, even though I was not allowed
to canvass it!

LOW-INCOME

The fifth place to start a bus route is in the low-income
ghetto areas. Now many of you will put on the brakes right
here. You are thinking that those people would not be welcome
in your church. Listen, God loves all kinds of people. We must
go to the ghetto. We must go, get the people from the ghetto,
and bring them in. This is an ideal place, if you want to fill a
bus quick. You will have a larger turnover. You will have a lot
of people who come for a week or two, then drop out for a
week or two, then show up again. They will be the most incon-
sistent, and undependable of all the people you will bring. Yet
you will reach many of them for Jesus. There may be a mixed
neighborhood, some black, some white, some you won't be sure

what. We go to everyone, and we bring anyone who wants to come, regardless of color, race or creed. We believe that Jesus loves all, regardless of color. In the ghetto areas you will find two, three or four families living in run-down houses, many in such terrible condition they ought to be condemned, and many of them have—but the people still live in them because they have no place else to go. We need to go and get these people out. Don't be afraid to walk up those shaky steps. Go all the way to the back apartment. Check every door in the building to see if anyone is living there. We have found as many as 38 people living in one large house—a former mansion. We were able to bring 21 out of one house. Don't neglect the ghettos. They need you, and Jesus died for them as much as for anyone else!

ABOVE CITY STORES

If you live in the city, look above the stores. Drive down the streets when the stores are closed after dark, and look for lights in the windows, or curtains blowing. It may be the owner of the store living upstairs, or it may be rented out. I recall being in the town of BelAir, Maryland. I suppose I had been by the hobby shop hundreds of times, and it had never occurred to me that someone might be living upstairs. That day I suggested to the bus pastor that we visit some of the people living over the stores. We went in and found a man about 70 years old. He was almost blind, and had never been to church in his life! His wife was about the same age. We tried to witness to him about his need of Jesus, but he had been to a lodge, and had some lodge religion. His wife kept saying, "Oh, he's alright, he'll make it okay." And things like, "You don't need to talk to him about going to Heaven—he's going to Heaven because he's a good man, and ain't never done nothing too wrong."

People are up above the stores, and they are blinded by sin and ignorance. Someone has got to reach them for Jesus. So ride down the street and look above the stores. Look in the alleys. Do you see cars parked there? Do you see lights on? Do you see a TV antenna? If so, someone lives there for whom Jesus died. Go to see them.

UPPER INCOME

Another place to run your buses is among the upper income homes of the city. Many churches have marked these places off as being too hard to reach. But few have really tried to reach these people. They are defeated before they start because they have convinced themselves the people will not come. They think that because a man has a Cadillac, an Olds and a Mustang in his driveway, he will not send his children to church on a bus. But these people feel more morally obligated to have their children in church, even though they won't take them themselves. When they promise to have the children ready, they are more likely to follow through than anyone else. When a rich parent says his children will be ready, they generally are ready. It will take a little longer to build a route among the upper-income families, but once built, it will be a very stable route. It will be consistent. So don't scratch off the doctors, lawyers and elite of your area. They will come, too, if you approach them right. The buses that have the highest averages in our church are running in the middle-to-upper income people.

FOLLOW SCHOOL BUS

One good way to find where the people live is to follow the school bus as it leaves the school. Every time it stops, mark the place and see how many get off. The next Saturday, when you go out to visit, visit every place the school bus stopped!

Selecting the routes is very important. If I were to start a new work, I would spend Mondays, Tuesdays and Wednesdays just riding around, spotting homes and areas where bus work would be good, and praying for the people. Pray for them even though you do not know them, or know their names. Begin to pray, and God will help you. As you leave the church on Saturday, mark down the time, note how long it takes to drive to the area, and you will know approximately how long it will take to drive the route on Sunday. Allow at least two minutes for each stop to pick up riders. If you make 15 stops, you can figure on at least 30 minutes of stop time, and maybe 30 minutes of drive time. If you try to keep your routes to about an hour's time, you will have enough time for a good program on the bus, and for promotion, and you will be able to cover enough ground to fill the bus.

You might try following the ice cream truck in the summertime. Since his salary depends on it, he is determined to know where the children are. Let him help you find the same children, although for a quite different reason.

GOVERNMENT INSTALLATIONS

Another place for a bus route is government installations such as bases for Army, Navy, Marines, or Coast Guard, etc. These are great places for a bus. We run 6 buses to Fort Knox, about 25 miles away. We had some opposition from some of the chaplains at first, but we began by visiting in the Vine Grove homes area on the base. But in getting there, we had to drive right by the government housing area on the base. So bus pastor "Slick" Goodman began to invite those whom he found standing by the side of the road, and they began to come. Finally, he had penetrated one of the subdivisions, and then another, until one day he brought a total of 338 from Fort Knox, a place we couldn't get into!

If there is a base near you, but you can't seem to get into it, get someone living on the base to write a letter to the Provost Marshal, asking that the bus be permitted to come onto the base and pick up their children for Sunday school. That will open the door for you. Then, for the first 10 or 15 families you pick up, have them write a letter asking that you come for them with the bus. Keep these letters handy in case you are challenged about coming on the base. If you develop a good relationship with the base commander, and the guards at the gate, you will have little trouble in just a short time. You probably will never need the letters. But if there is a change of command, or some new chaplains come who complain, the letter will come in handy to justify your position, and your activity. If you can, try to work out some special programs such as choir presentations, Christmas or Easter programs in the base chapel. This will build good will with those on the base, and make your bus pastor's job a lot easier.

Selecting the routes is important, so look before you leap. A wise choice will bring great benefits. A poor choice will bring headaches.

PART III
WORKERS YOU NEED

CHAPTER 13
THE BUS DIRECTOR

First of all, a bus director must be called of God to his work. He must believe that it is something God wants him to do. There are many men in many churches who could become really good bus directors with the proper training, experience and guidance. But there must be the conviction that it is God's will for a man to serve as a bus director.

Let me tell you about Jim Layman. Jim was an ordinary layman in our church. He was owner of the Layman-Walker Equipment Company in Louisville. He was a successful business man, and a member of Beth Haven Baptist Church. But he felt a desire to get into the bus ministry, and serve as a bus pastor. Jim became a bus pastor, and went at it with a lot of zeal and determination to get the job done. Then he felt the call of God upon his life.

About that same time, a pastor called from California. He asked me to come to his church as bus director, but I told him "NO" because I knew I was serving where God wanted me, and had no indication that God wanted me to move. "Well, do you have a recommendation for someone who could serve as our bus director?" he asked. I told him there were two men in our church who could do the job. Jim Layman was one of them. The other was the preacher in our Junior age church.

The pastor felt that Jim would be the man for their church since they had a Junior Church Director, and did not want a conflict. They contacted Jim, and he felt this was God's will for him. He then sold his business, his home, and moved his family to California! The church was bringing in about 400-450 each week on their buses. Jim went there in June, 1971, and six months later, there were upwards of 1900 coming on the buses! Jim was an ordinary layman, but became an excellent bus director.

All over the country I get calls asking for men to serve as bus directors. But there are very few men around who have the training and the experience to qualify as good bus directors. So we are beginning a Bus Directors School at Beth Haven Baptist Church, in Louisville, to train men in how to be effective bus directors in local churches.

A bus director is just as important to a church as a music director, education director or assistant pastor. This man's job is to reach people for Jesus, and lead the people in doing the same thing. Music and education will reach some people, but a bus director will reach more people in one year's time than all the other ministries combined will in ten years time! You cannot have a good bus ministry without a good music program, and a good educational program, but it is the bus director who will bring the people in to gain the benefit from these programs. All these work together for the one purpose of winning lost souls to faith in Jesus Christ.

The bus director is not the pastor of the church, and cannot take his place in any way. But the pastor has a load on him already, and he should give the laymen in his church a chance to reach people for Jesus. The bus director becomes the in-between-man for the pastor in motivating and directing the people to reach their community for Chirst.

THE BUS DIRECTORS CALL

FEEL CALLED

1. A bus director must feel that he has been called to do this work.

BEEN A BUS PASTOR

2. A bus director must have first been a bus pastor himself. How can you tell someone else what to do, when you have never done it yourself? A bus director cannot hope to train others, unless he has first experienced the problems himself. He cannot get good programs together, or the teenagers inspired unless he has first been there.

I wouldn't want to put a man on the battle line until he had first had some basic training. The same holds true in regard to a bus director. To take a man who has the potential to become a good bus director, but who lacks training and experience, and put him in charge of the bus ministry is to invite disaster. He will soon begin to falter and wilt under the pressures, and will quit—all because he did not have enough training and experience to lead others adequately, and understand the needs of the work himself.

GOALS SET FOR LIFE

3. A bus director must have goals set for his life. He must be one who intends to do something. The goal might be for 100 people to come on the buses each week. But at the same time, there must be the ultimate goal of reaching thousands of people.

My goal is to have 5,000 people coming on 100 buses by 1974. I believe this is possible, as soon as we have the buildings to put the people in. We now run 20 buses, with an average of about 70 per bus.

MUST INSPIRE OTHERS

4. A bus director must be one to inspire others. He should have a regular bus pastors meeting, or a time when he meets with his people. He must be able to inspire them to attempt great things for God. And he must be a man who can take the Word of God, and speak with authority from it for the benefit and spiritual growth of the workers he directs. He must be able to challenge them to do things they have never done before. He must be one who can rejoice with them in victory, anguish with them when things don't go right, and keep them from becoming discouraged when the attacks of Satan become strong.

BE ABLE TO TAKE PRESSURE

5. The bus director must be one who can take pressure. He gets caught between the enthusiasm of the bus workers, and the practical instructions from the pastor. The pastor may come in one day, right after you have really whipped up a head of enthusiasm, and say, "We are going to have to slow up a little bit. We are expanding too rapidly for the rest of the church to

keep up. So let's just hold what we have for awhile, and later push on." Now, how do you keep up morale, and keep the workers enthusiastic for their work, and at the same time tell them not to bring in too many new ones?

First of all, you must do what the pastor says. He is the pastor, and is the head of the church. Always do what the pastor says. God has appointed him to be head over the work, and not you.

Second, I'm going to have my bus pastors concentrate on getting their routes thoroughly organized, and spend some more time on training the workers in doing a more efficient job. Maybe we'll try to recruit and train new workers.

Thirdly, use the time to engage in a deeper level of training for the people who are already doing a good job. This way, while we are in a delay period, we are using the time profitably. Then, when we can really get going again, we'll be better able to do it.

CHAPTER 14
THE BUS PASTOR

The bus pastor is a very unusual person. In one year's time the average bus pastor will bring more people to a saving knowledge of Jesus Christ, than the pastors of many churches. The bus pastor is unusual in that he is willing to give time every Saturday to visit, enlist riders, prepare bus programs, and bring people to the Lord Jesus Christ. What kind of person is a good bus pastor? Here are some characteristics:

First, he must be a born-again believer in Christ. I do not want someone to pastor a bus route who is not saved, or who does not know for sure whether he is going to Heaven or not. How could such a one give spiritual guidance and counseling? No, I believe a person must be saved before they become a bus pastor.

Secondly, he must be dedicated to the work of the Lord, and surrendered to the call of God for bus work. He must be willing to sacrifice, and give some time to God that he has not been giving. Every bus pastor must be willing to give at least 3 hours every Saturday to visit on his route. There may be other days when he visits, but Saturday is the main day for bus visitation. He will not wash his car on Saturday, get a haircut or go on a picnic. He will not stay home to watch ballgames, or other events. A bus pastor is one who cuts all the strings, and gives every Saturday to God.

We require our bus pastor to visit a minimum of 3 hours every Saturday. I have a theory that for every hour of visiting on Saturday, he will have 10 riders on Sunday. So if the bus pastor visits three hours, he will have thirty people. If he visits four hours, he will have forty people, and so on. But if he visits nine hours, he will not have ninety, but ninety-five people. This is because God is not cheap, and gives time-and-a-half overtime for everything over 8 hours!

A man once visited our church to go out with our bus pastors. In the bus pastors meeting I mentioned that for every hour of visiting, 10 riders would come. This pastor said, "You'll have to

prove that to me—I just don't believe it." So I sent him out with
one of our bus pastors, and the two of them visited for nine
hours. When they came back to the meeting that Saturday
night, the pastor said, "I still don't think we have seen enough
people to have 100 on the bus tomorrow." Well, when the bus
came in to Sunday school the next day, there were over 100
people on it! That pastor became a believer! Every hour of
visiting on Saturday, means 10 riders on Sunday! He went back
to his home church, and the following Saturday two teams of
men went out visiting to enlist riders. The two teams visited for
nine hours in a subdivision. They only had one bus, and when
they took it out Sunday morning, a sea of humanity was waiting
to get on. Over 200 people were waiting to get on that one 60-
passenger bus!

Many of our men have proven this to be true. Over 20 of our
bus pastors have brought in 100 or more on a Sunday morning.
As you walk down the halls of Beth Haven Baptist Church, you
will see the pictures of the bus pastors who have sacrificed,
given their Saturdays to God, and are in our "100 Hall of Fame."

The bus pastor must be willing to sacrifice on Sunday, too. For
the average bus pastor, Sunday begins at 7:00 a.m. That's when
he gets up to call his driver and workers so they will be ready
to go out on time. He will pick up his bus team, and make the
route. Then, after church is over, he will take the riders back
home, take his workers back home, and then he can go home
himself. Most bus pastors return to their own homes about 2:00
in the afternoon. If he runs his bus on Sunday night, he will go
out again around 5 o'clock in order to have the riders at church
for the Training Hour at 6:15. When the evening service is over
(about 8:30 or 9:00), he will take his riders home, and then go
home himself. It's usually about 11:00 before the bus pastor gets
home on Sunday night. A good bus pastor must be willing to
sacrifice his weekends for the glory of God, and the winning of
the lost.

DUTIES

What are the duties of a bus pastor? First, he must visit his
route every week. That means he visits every rider every week.
Secondly, he must spend time enlisting new riders very week.

If a bus pastor fails to visit at least 15 new homes every week, it won't be long before the number of riders will begin to go down. Thirdly, the bus pastor must maintain order on his bus. Neighborhoods will vary, but usually the children from the upper income homes will behave very well. But regardless of what neighborhood they come from, there will always be one or two who will be disorderly, and want to jump over the seats, or fight, or what have you. And the bus pastor must maintain order on the bus. One of our bus pastors runs his route in a ghetto area where there are some rival gangs. And these rival gangs ride the bus—at the same time! This bus pastor carries his Bible with him, and also a large paddle. The paddle is inscribed with the words, "Love and Peace." He loves those kids, but if they don't behave, they get a piece! The kids on this route love the bus pastor, and he brings an average of 75 each week, and has done so for over a year!

The bus pastor must maintain order, or his riders will stop coming. Parents will not allow their children to come if injuries and danger are common. And the children will not want to come if they cannot enjoy the bus ride because of trouble on the bus.

Then, it is the bus pastor's responsibility to maintain a good program on the bus. Usually he will have a teenage helper in charge of presenting the program, but it is the bus pastor's responsibility to be sure that teenager is prepared each Sunday morning with a good program on the bus. We will deal more with the program themselves in a separate chapter.

Another duty of the bus pastor is to lead people to Jesus Christ. I firmly believe that bus pastors should be soul-winners. They should seek to win people individually, and in groups as when on the bus. A good bus pastor should know how to give an invitation on the bus. By this I mean he should be able to get down on his knees in the front of the bus and show the riders how he received Christ.

We have talked about the life of the bus pastor, and the duties of the bus pastor. Let's now turn to the rewards of the bus pastor. I believe bus pastors will receive rewards for getting people saved. It is a great reward here on earth to see people from your bus route saved each Sunday. Our bus pastors fill out a report each Sunday night, and part of it tells how many were saved that day. There are often 6 or 7 names listed, and as many as 15 have been saved from one bus route on a single Sunday! The bus pastor is also rewarded by seeing lives changed. There are people now in schools studying for the ministry who were saved on bus routes. Some are now on the mission field who were saved on a bus route. Parents have come together, love has been restored, homes have been changed because a bus pastor cared enough to give his best.

Another reward is for a bus pastor to see his church double, or triple in attendance. In a church that is already running 3,000 it may be hard for him to see that, but in smaller churches, where there is no bus ministry, one man can double its attendance! He will do part of it himself on his route, and he will inspire others to do it on other routes. In such cases, it will not be long until the church actually doubles its average attendance. Ronald Sturgil has brought as many on one bus route, as what the church had in total attendance before going into bus evangelism in Bel Air, Maryland. One bus pastor in Davenport, Iowa, brought 287 from one bus route one Sunday. The previous year, the church averaged 76 in Sunday school! Yes, one good bus pastor can actually double some churches himself. And when he trains others to be good bus pastors, he is responsible for doubling, tripling, or even more.

But as great as are the rewards here, I believe God has some even greater rewards for those who become bus pastors, and pay the price necessary to bring great numbers of people to the church to hear the Word of God, and be saved.

CHAPTER 15
THE TEENAGE STEWARDESS
by a bus stewardess at Beth Haven

In July, 1969, my father became a bus pastor. Since I was a teenager, and he needed a bus helper, I got "drafted" in the work. Within a month I learned the songs, and got to know the people who rode the bus. Sometimes I would go out on Saturdays and visit along with my father.

I enjoyed being a bus helper. I learned a lot about human relations, and about life in general. And I learned to have a concern for other people. But my biggest problem during that first year-and-one-half was that I had not yet come to a saving knowledge of Jesus Christ. I played the game of church! My advice to anyone who wants to be a bus helper is to make sure you are saved. Secondly, you should want to serve the Lord. If you are not really interested in being a bus helper, don't be one just to say you are doing it. The children who come on the bus need your love and help. You must love and care for people, and you can't do that properly until you have been saved.

You should have some type of program on your bus. This helps the children and adults learn about Jesus, and it usually keeps them in their seats and out of trouble. The program I use includes a lot of songs, and question and answer games. Make up a song list and always have it handy. There are many songs you can sing, but keep a list so you will know what has already been used, and what everyone knows. At times I have lost the song list, and made the mistake of asking the children what they wanted to sing. Almost without exception, a small argument developed over what song we would sing, and what song we would sing *first!* Things like that can cause a problem, but are easily avoided if you just keep the song list handy. For the question and answer games, I do it just like we were in a classroom. They can take turns answering, or have one side against the other, or just raise their hand to answer. At times they may receive a lollipop for answering a question, or the one answering the most questions may get some reward.

On Promotion Days, help the bus pastor in any way possible *the day before.* Sometimes we will make popcorn, or cookies, or maybe something else on the Saturday before a Promotion Day. And be sure to get lots of rest the day before a big Promotion Day, because the unexpected will surely happen, and you will need a clear head to think and react properly. To say nothing of the extra energy that will be needed to handle a larger-than-usual crowd!

Every October our church has a Round-Up Day. From July to October we had not had a hundred on our bus, and we were kind of discouraged. The most up until that time was into the sixties. So when Round-Up Sunday week came, we went all-out on promotion and visitation. Dad had handbills to hand out on the route, and he started knocking on doors. He enlisted the help of other regular riders to call or visit in whatever way they could. My brother (also a teenager) helped visit. During the day I made cookies. That night we popped popcorn and bagged it. Our goal was high and we were determined to make it. Dad had something for everyone who rode the bus, and a special gift for the mothers who came. We all welcomed the bed that night!

The bus arrived at our house at 8:15 a.m. to start picking up. Mother drove the car to church with all the cookies, popcorn and prizes. Before the route was half finished, the bus was full. At least it looked full to me. We still had more to pick up, but couldn't fit them in the bus. Dad called the church for another bus. We went on to the church while Dad waited for the second bus. The singing that morning was tremendous!

When we arrived at the church, other buses were pulling in packed full. As we counted the people getting off our bus, we were really happy when the count went past 100. And we almost shouted when the last person got off. We were amazed. We had 130 people on a 60-passenger bus! We were even happier when the second bus pulled in, and 22 more got off! The total for our bus route that day was 152! What a great time we had! We put some of the people in the less-crowded bus going home, so it was more comfortable for them.

You are asking, "How did you get 130 people on one bus?" Well, we had 8 and 9 in some seats. It was so crowded that it was impossible for anyone to fall down! I feel the Lord led us in it, and really blessed us. Dad was so happy, he was ready to turn cartwheels!

A bus helper should always work with the bus pastor and the bus driver. You are to be a helper, not a hindrance. You are to be an example to the people who ride the bus. Greet the people as they come on the bus. Compliment them, and get them to smile. You should always be smiling. Not just with your mouth, either, but with your eyes, too! Don't be a fake. People know when it's not real.

When the bus pastor is not on the bus for some reason, you should be able to get the bus program running smoothly. You should get off the bus and make sure the children get across the street safely, and without trouble. If a person needs assistance, help him. This is just common courtesy. At times the children will fight. The best way to control this is to separate the ones who are fighting, whether they are fighting physically, or just vocally.

There will be days when you think nothing is going right. Remember, Satan does not want you to have a part in getting a lot of people saved, and will do all he can to discourage you. One summer I had to start a brand new bus route. It was hard getting to know the people, learning the songs they knew, and teaching them the songs I knew. I was really discouraged at times. Then two Sundays in a row, one of the children got sick on the bus. I had my roll of paper towels with me, and cleaned up the mess, but it sure didn't do much for my morale! Always try to get a sick child to the front of the bus, so he can be the first one off when you get to the church, and get whatever help he needs. And try to have a first-aid kit on the bus. You'll need it sooner or later!

Always keep an eye out for those kids who want to stick their heads, arms, elbows, hands or whatever else they can manage out the windows. If a child persists in it, close the window, or make him sit somewhere else—preferably near you! Many children like to stand on the seats, or twist into the most unbelievable shapes. This is dangerous and must be stopped. Always make them stay in their seats. You just have to be on the watch all the time, because there is no way to know what might happen. You surely can't just relax and enjoy the ride!

You don't have to be a good singer to be a bus helper. You do need to carry a tune, and be loud. Make sure you know the songs well before you try to teach them to the children. And all the songs you sing should be Christian oriented. Sometimes one of the children will want to sing a popular song, but you must not allow it. They have come to learn about Jesus and God's Word, so keep the songs in line with that purpose. Sing the songs on your list to yourself constantly to keep them fresh in your mind. On the bus, announce each song before you sing it, and find out how many already know it. This will tell you if you have to teach it first, or can go ahead and sing it with lots of enthusiasm. No one likes group singing if the group doesn't sing!

Usually we start the singing when we get close to our last pick-up. This way, you can greet everyone and talk with everyone before the singing starts. Halfway to church, ask who has had a birthday during the week. Then sing "Happy Birthday" for them.

Go through the Bible and make up questions from familiar Bible stories. Write them down, along with the answers. That way you won't be embarrassed by a sudden lapse of memory. A good idea is to ask the riders to read a certain portion of the Bible, then ask the questions from that portion the following week. This way the riders will get interested in the Scriptures and read all they can. It will also help you to read more of the Bible! Whatever you do, stress Bible reading in every way you can.

While the bus driver is parking the bus, the bus pastor will pray, or ask someone else to pray. Help the children get quiet and in a prayerful attitude just before you arrive at the church. Songs such as "Thank You, Lord," "Turn Your Eyes Upon Jesus," or "Whisper A Prayer" will help greatly in getting them quiet and in an attitude of prayer.

One word should sum up your own personal life: DEDICA-TION! You should be dedicated to serving the Lord through your prayer, social life, and Bible reading. Yes, I said through your social life, too! Your social life will tell what kind of person you really are. Who you hang around with, what you say, where you go, and your moods will tell a lot about you.

If a person hangs around with a wild crowd, that person usually is wild, too. But even if he isn't, people will think he is because of the people he associates with. Christians should associate with other Christians! You should be sure to go to church faithfully, serve the Lord joyfully, and witness to the lost as much as you can.

After church is over, as we go back home, we have the drawings for prizes, or give out the suckers. There is a program on the bus going home, too, and it is important, because it is the last thing the riders will remember from that morning. Make the programs interesting, but simple.

The bus helper has two main jobs: keeping the children entertained, and making sure they behave. If the children are properly entertained, they will behave. So keep it interesting!

CHAPTER 16

THE WIFE OF THE BUS PASTOR/BUS DIRECTOR

By Alice Gentry

Perhaps you men will allow me to have this part of the book to share with your wives a few helpful hints, a few pitfalls, and a heap of spiritual blessings that will be their lot as the wife of a bus pastor, or bus director.

One Sunday night in October, 1963, as we sat in the Highland Park Baptist Church, Chattanooga, Tennessee, a white-haired man named M. J. Parker climbed the pew directly in back of my husband and me during an invitation, and gently put his hands on each of our shoulders. He prayed that God would use us in the bus ministry. Before we realized what was happening, we found ourselves actively involved in knocking on doors, and inviting people to ride the bus to church. Not knowing much more than a few Bible verses, and our own conversion experience, I felt very unqualified in this new work. But in spite of our inadequacies, God seemed to bless every fumbling effort we made for Him. Little is much when God is in it!

It only took a short time for the full commitment of bus evangelism to hit me. Suddenly I realized that Saturdays were no longer our own. I must admit the "old nature" really got in the way, and wanted to rebel. I thought about complaining to my husband that the work was *just too hard,* and required *just too much* of our time. But I didn't. Then there were the times when he would take our last dollar and give it to someone in dire need —as if we weren't! Again, the "old nature" would flare up, and I would feel sorry for myself because the dollar wasn't spent on something we needed. And every Sunday morning, Sunday night and Wednesday night we rode the bus to pick up the riders and bring them to the services. Not only did we bring them to the services, but we also had to sit with them (50 to 100 children and teenagers), and pacify them during the service! My, how that "old nature" bugged me during those times. I looked at other couples sitting together, absorbing all the good preaching without any distraction, while we had to give our attention to all those riders. After all, weren't we there in Tennessee Temple Bible School to study and prepare for God's service? Why did we have to look after everybody, and his brother?

At first I did not feel the same way toward the bus ministry as my husband. But I slowly realized that my calling was jointly with his, and because I was to be in subjection to him as the head of our home and family, his calling was mine also. After submitting myself in full surrender to God, and in subjection to my husband, a compelling force broke through my heart. And with it came a driving zeal to work, and a sincere love for the people.

I found myself bringing home little dirty children, and bathing them while my heart ached and wept inside because of the conditions in which they had to live. I shall never forget one six-year old boy I bathed. Upon seeing his clean skin he was fascinated, and rubbed his legs saying, "Oh, my skin is so smooth and soft now!" And he commented about the clean walls, and the running water inside the house. You see, chickens were allowed to roost in his house. And an old icebox in the kitchen section of the one-room shanty was so dirty, the children could carve names in the filth, and fill in the letters with lipstick!

My heart ached for those who wore 3 and 4 sets of clothing (scarcely changing them for weeks) at one time, in order to keep warm in the winter. And they slept on iron beds of filthy rags. Many times we smelled the odor of pinto beans and fat back, plus the coal smoke from the crude indoor fireplaces. Sometimes the stench of urine-soaked cots and clothes would be almost unbearable. But God was ever faithful to give the needed grace to visit these homes, and offer whatever spiritual and material help we could.

Then came the time when two young girls were dumped in our home with a trunk of clothes, because the parents were not capable of caring for them. I remember vividly the feeble elderly who sometimes begged us to stay, just to have fellowship with someone. Some were dying with cancer. Some had the various problems and diseases that come with age. But all brought to my heart the impact of the brevity of life, and the certainty of death, and the urgency of getting out the gospel.

As I sit here in the comfort and security of our home, I am reminded of an older couple I shall call Minnie and George. My husband and another bus pastor found them living in a tent in the woods during the cold winter months. Minnie had lost the use of her legs in an accident. The men secured a wheelchair for her, and found them a small house to live in. George pushed Minnie up and down the road in that wheelchair until the rubber was completely chewed off the wheels. But the greatest thing about this couple that no one else seemed to care about is that they both found Christ as their Saviour!

Perhaps by now you are thinking, "No, that type of ministry is not for me. I could never lower myself to visit in homes such as you have described, or bring those kind of children into my home." You probably have never had a poor child nestle up to you, and say, "You smell so good. I wish my Mommie smelled like you." Or, "I wish I had you and Brother Gardiner for my Mom and Dad." I remember during the early months in the bus ministry I wore a beautiful white coat, with a large white silver fur collar. It was a gift from my husband. But the kids hugged my neck so much, and felt the softness of that fur collar so often, that a cleaning job was needed almost weekly—and soon they had literally plucked a hole right in the back center of that fur collar!

The bus ministry cannot be called glamorous, or easy. It is the hardest work I ever engaged in, but there is much glory in it for the Lord, if we let Him receive the glory! There is much excitement in the work, if we have the right attitude. And there are tremendous blessings regularly, if we major on the souls saved, and minor on the hardships involved!

October 1972 marked our 9th anniversary in the bus ministry, and I can honestly say there are no regrets, or reservations concerning the commitment I made some 8 years ago to follow my Lord and my husband in this beloved ministry. Maybe you who have children fear they will not fit into this type of ministry. Maybe you have reservations about them coming into contact with poorer children. Let me tell you that our daughter was five years old when we began the work. She dearly loved it. The bus rides were exciting, and inspiring, and she fit in perfectly with other children. They treated her like a little queen, and she, in turn, begged to take them to our home. Many times we took her with us on Saturday visitation, and because of her we were able to reach more people. A few times when I had to visit on the bus route alone, she was along, and served as a real helper and prayer partner in finding the homes.

May I stress the fact that the bus ministry does not only reach and serve lower class people, it also attracts middle and upper-income people, too. We are now working in a church where many refined people ride the bus, and some are now co-laborers in this ministry. It has been some time since I have visited in a home, or found children outwardly equal to those in the early years of our ministry. God first placed us among the most needy and helpless group of people I have ever seen to do His work of winning souls. He used those people to break our hearts, in order that we might have compassion upon all men, regardless of race, creed, color, education or culture. Although there is not the outward evidence of filth and poverty among the people we now minister to, we know there is inside evidence of an unclean heart waiting for someone to bring the remedy that will cure and clean away all sin. As one teenager commented after accepting Christ, "I feel so clean now!"

My husband is now a bus director, and God is using him here at home. But He has also seen fit to thrust him out into the field of helping other churches across the country establish effective bus ministries. Church bus evangelism will never be great without a lot of hard work, and prayer. And a bus pastor needs a loving and encouraging wife, willing to pay the cost that lost souls will be saved. Ladies, are you willing to surrender all to God? Be in subjection to your husband? Sacrifice Saturdays, as well as Sundays for God's work? Be understanding when your husband must visit on other days of the week? Or when he has to cancel a very important dinner date with you because of an emergency call? When he puts off doing odd jobs around the house? When he has to put others first, and you and the children second? When he gives financially under God's leading, even though you wouldn't do it that way?

Will you take the initiative in leading family devotions when your husband is engaged in a night prayer meeting, or when he is out of town, or when he is late in visiting homes? Can you face criticism with kindness and boldness when church leaders (and members) criticize your husband's mannerisms, education, motives and techniques in bus evangelism? Can you absorb, or pass off, the criticism of church workers when the increases in attendance requires extra work, and adjustments in the church program? And when they blame your husband because he is doing his job well? It takes a willing heart, and a determined attitude to do all these things. Yet God has promised, and will give the victory over these attacks of Satan. And you'll find it's worth every bit of it, and more!

PART IV
ABOUT THE BUSES

CHAPTER 17
FINANCING THE BUS MINISTRY

This is an important subject for churches that are considering bus evangelism. Some think bus evangelism so expensive that they never begin at all. But there are several ways of financing a bus evangelism ministry that are workable.

THROUGH INDIVIDUALS

There may be someone in your church who could give $1500.00 to $2000.00 for a bus. Some churches have several people in them who purchase the buses as they are needed.

THROUGH GROUPS

The men's group in a church will often take this as a special project. The men will have money in bank accounts that God wants to use. Often the men's group of the church will buy the first bus. Another group that could buy a bus is the women's group in the church. There is not a better way to do missionary activity than providing a bus to bring people in to hear the gospel so they can be saved.

THE JUNIOR DEPARTMENT

At Beth Haven we financed our second and third bus primarily through the Junior department. They challenged the teenage and adult department to buy a bus. The Junior department was out to win. Those kids sold pop bottles and begged their parents for nickels and dimes. They brought in anywhere from $50.00 to $100.00 per week toward purchasing the bus. In the hallway we had the outlines of three buses. Each part of the bus was worth a certain amount of money. The fender cost so much, the windows cost so much, etc. As the money from each department came in, the parts of the buses were shaded in. The Junior department had their bus paid for by the time the teen had the front bumper, front tires and hood paid for. The adults had only half their bus paid for. The Juniors had challenged each other: boys against girls as to who could bring in the most each week. We made a giant see-saw with buckets on each. One end had a red bucket, the other end had a blue bucket. The see-saw was held in place by a pin. After each side had put in all their money in the buckets, the pin was pulled and whichever side weighed the most would go down and set off a whistle if it was the girls side, or a siren if the boys had won. There was lots of excitement each week to see which side would win. And the Junior department out-did both the teens and the adults!

BUS BANKS

These are little cardboard banks in the shape of a bus. They are available through Church Bus Evangelism Supply, Box 90361, Nashville, Tennessee. On a Sunday morning, the ushers will have a good supply of these bus banks assembled. Then the pastor will ask the congregation, "How many of you would give one penny for a child to come on one of our buses to Sunday school and church?" Almost everyone will raise their hand. Then the pastor will ask, "How many of you would give one penny for *each* one who will come on one of our buses to Sunday school and church?" Again, many will raise their hands. Then the pastor says, "All right, now just keep your hand raised until the ushers give you a bus bank." From that time onward, the pastor need only announce each Sunday the number of riders for that day. Then each person who is participating in this program will put one cent in the bus bank for each person riding the bus. So if you had 50 riders that day, each one would put 50 cents in his bus bank. The following week 106 people ride the buses. So each participant puts $1.06 in his bus bank. Suppose on the third Sunday 227 riders come in, and $2.27 goes into the bus banks. Then on the fourth week, only 210 riders come, so $2.10 goes into each bank. At the end of the four weeks you have

raised $6.01 per bus bank. If you had 100 people participating in
the bus bank program, you would have over $600.00 for your
bus evangelism program! This will easily pay for all the operating expenses, and provide a continuing balance toward the purchase of your next bus.

When we first began our bus ministry at Beth Haven we gave
out bus banks on Thanksgiving Day weekend. We asked our
people to bring them back at Christmas completely filled as a
Christmas gift to the Lord. We received over $3,000.00 in that
one month's time which carried our bus work for some time
afterward.

Another way to use the bus banks is for each family to take
one home, and each member of the family must put something
in the bus bank before each meal. In an average family of five,
the total in the bank will be more than you, or they, thought
they could ever give.

CHURCH BUDGET

The church will need to appropriate between $600.00 and
$900.00 each year per bus for operation, maintenance and
insurance costs. This will vary from place to place, and will
depend upon the number of buses, how often they are run, the
distance travelled and the mechanical condition of the buses.
You must also figure in the cost of hiring a mechanic, if you
do that.

FAITH PROMISE

In this we ask people to promise to give a certain amount
above and beyond what they normally do. For instance, if a
man's tithe was $20.00 per week, and his offering above the
tithe was $4.00 per week, he would normally be giving $24.00
per week. But if he makes a faith promise for an additional
$2.00 per week for bus evangelism, then he will give $26.00
per week. But he is not obligated to give the extra $2.00 unless
God somehow supplies it first to him! I do not ask people to
readjust their other payments in order to fulfill this faith
promise. Let me illustrate. A day laborer in my Sunday school
class made a faith promise of $2.00 per week. He Simply

promised God that if God would give him $2.00 extra, he would give it for the bus ministry. When Friday afternoon came there was no increase in his paycheck, just the same as he always got. He took his wife to the grocery store, and he found a parking place and waited while she went in to the shop. In a few minutes another lady came out of the store with two bags of groceries which she set down on the sidewalk. She went back into the store and came out again with two more bags of groceries which she set down by the others. She kept looking up and down the driveway, evidently expecting someone to come and pick her up. After some time had passed, she came over to where this man was sitting in his car, and said, "Excuse me, but I have called a taxi to take me home, but they have not come. My butter is beginning to melt and the frozen things are starting to thaw out. I live just a few blocks from here. Would you mind giving me a lift?" Well, he wondered how it would look if his wife saw him drive off with a strange woman in his car, and he was about to refuse when it seemed the Lord said, "Here is your faith promise." So he took the lady and her groceries to her home. As he was about to leave the lady opened her purse and said, "I usually pay the taxi man $2.00 for this. Will you accept it, please?" He said, "Thank you" to the lady, and "Thank you" to the Lord, and hurried back to the grocery store parking lot, where his space was still open. God had supplied his faith promise, and I could give many more instances of how similar things have happened. The faith promise plan is one of the best ways I know to finance bus evangelism. There is no scheming, no planning, no figuring. It is simply promising God that if He will give you something extra, you will give it back to Him for the winning of souls through bus evangelism. At Beth Haven our faith promises now give over $1,000.00 per month to support our bus ministry.

THE RIDERS

If a bus averages 50 to 60 riders per week, and they are properly motivated, that bus will bring in from $15.00 to $25.00 per week from the riders. You may want to check from time to time, and encourage the riders to try to increase their giving.

THROUGH SOUL WINNING

When I had been at Beth Haven about six months, I asked the pastor if I could start a Sunday school class. I wanted to call it the Bible Class. He said it would be fine, so we went out and won two people. We began teaching them, and then won two more. We taught them, and they went out and won some more. In just three years time that class now averages over 100 adults per Sunday. It came about through soul-winning, but the offering from that one class could support our bus ministry. You should always try to win souls, but God may use this as the means of bringing into your church people who will give generously to your bus evangelism program.

MISSIONS BUDGET

Some churches include this in their missions outreach budget. By doing this you can easily see what effect this giving is having, and how souls are being reached with the gospel.

These are a few ways of financing bus evangelism. Some people say it won't pay for itself. The reason they say that is because they have not really gotten down to planning how to make it pay. Last year our bus ministry at Beth Haven cost close to $80,000.00. But it was entirely paid for through the bus ministry itself. It's really a matter of "ask and ye shall receive." God may not supply everything we want, but He will supply everything that we need. Ask God to supply your bus evangelism ministry, and He will!

CHAPTER 18
INSURING THE BUS

Always be sure all buses are fully insured from the moment they become the legal property of the church.

THE INSURANCE BINDER

The church has located three buses and intend to go the next day and pick them up. You may not have all the serial numbers, classification numbers, the year make and model, but call your insurance agent anyway. He can issue a binder which will cover the buses until you get back and give him all the details.

AMOUNTS OF COVERAGE

You will need $100,000.00 per person; $300,000.00 per accident; $50,000.00 property damage; and $2,000.00 medical payment. You should also carry uninsured motorist coverage. As of June, 1972, our church was paying $67.80 per bus per year for these coverages. There are many insurance companies that have a good church bus policy, but I will mention three because I have had experience with them: M.F.A. is our present insurance company. Preferred Risk Mutual is a non-drinkers company, and Nationwide Insurance Company also has a good church bus policy.

When you call your insurance company, *do not* say, "We have bought a school bus, and want to have it insured." Always say "We have purchased a *church* bus, and would like you to *give us a bid* on the cost of insurance." Make your insurance agent know he is competing with other companies for your business, and you will get a better price!

FLEET INSURANCE

Fleet insurance is available after you own five or more buses. Then there is an even larger discount after 10 buses, and a maximum discount when a church has 15 or more buses. At present, I know of no company that gives additional discounts beyond 15 buses.

The companies you contact regarding insurance for your buses will also want to bid on your church buildings and parsonage. Let them make a total bid for all your church insurance, as well as separate bids for each individual item. You may save enough money to buy another bus. And be sure to get bids, even if there is a member of the church in the insurance business. He will want the church's account, and may try to discourage getting bids from several companies. When I first started to get bus insurance here at Beth Haven, I called our agent (a member of the church) and told him I wanted to insure the bus. The cost: $260.00 per year. We added another bus, then another, and yet another. Each one cost us $260.00 per year for insurance. Since we put our insurance out for bid, we are paying almost $200.00 per year less per bus!

REPORT ALL ACCIDENTS

Report all accidents immediately to the bus director. He should call the insurance company right away. The faster the insurance man is on the scene, the better off you will be. If you delay an accident report, the victim will be more irritated and may press for higher damage claim. And your rates may go up.

COMPREHENSIVE INSURANCE

Should a church use comprehensive insurance on Sunday school evangelism buses? I would say "NO." Use regular insurance, but do not insure the bus itself for damage to its own windows, fenders or bumpers. It would cost too much for these old buses. If you have brand-new buses, get $100.00 deductible, but don't insure the older buses. If you carry Comprehensive insurance, be careful about making claims for vandalism. Each time you make a claim for repair, your rate may go up. And you may find that the rate will go up for all your buses, not just for the one that was damaged. I generally stay away from Comprehensive insurance.

RATE INCREASES

Expect increases every two or three years. Almost every company will do this. If the rate increase seems great, shop around for other companies who may give a better rate. Some people

don't like the idea of changing insurance companies, but I am
out to get the best coverage I can for the least amount of money.
Just always be sure that every bus you own is insured from the
time you get it until the time you get rid of it.

SHOULD OTHERS USE YOUR BUSES?

What if some other group wants to use, or rent your buses for
some activity? Check this carefully with your insurance company. Also, be sure to find out what limitations are on your
insurance. Some companies will insure only for one trip per
week. Policies will change from time to time and you'll have to
keep up with it each time.

HOW DO YOU PAY?

Some companies want full annual payment in one lump sum.
Others will set up quarterly or semi-annual payments. Some companies will insure the buses for 90 running days per year. This
provides insurance for 52 Sundays, your Vacation Bible School
and a few extra activities. This cuts down the rates, but it also
cuts down the use you have of the buses. But very few churches
will use their buses more than 90 days per year.

CHAPTER 19
RENOVATING, PAINTING AND LETTERING BUSES

The first thing to do is prepare the bus for the people. Scrub the bus inside and out with Fantastic cleaner. It's available in almost all grocery stores, but be sure to wear rubber gloves when you use it. The Fantastic cleaner will take off almost any kind of dirt except for tar. Scrub the inside of the bus, but *do not use a hose* to flush it out. The water will get under the linoleum flooring and cause it to curl up. So it will catch on the heels of shoes, and come up in big pieces. Then, if you want to put a new floor in, you will find you will have to wire-brush all the rust out that has come about from the water you have splashed down. So do not use a water hose in the bus. Scrub each section separately with the Fantastic, and then sponge it off. Scrub down the ceiling first, then the walls. Next do the seats. They can be removed and scrubbed outside the bus and hosed off. Then use Spic And Span to clean the floor of the bus. Scrub and clean the floor real good, then be sure the floor is thoroughly dry. The final step is to apply a coating of the kind of sealer used on gymnasium floors or on bowling alleys. A half-gallon of this sealer will protect the floor of the bus. It ought to be done at least once a year.

When you come to the outside of the bus, again be sure to scrub off all the grime and dirt. But especially be sure to get off all the tar that accumulates from road use. If you don't the tar will "bleed" right through the paint, and your bus will not look good. Then scrub the bus with Naptha cleaner. This will prepare the bus for the first coat of paint. We use Sherwin-Williams Ken-Gloss enamel to paint our buses. We currently pay about $6.00 per gallon, and it takes a gallon and a half to put one coat on a bus. We do not put two coats of paint on our buses. Usually a yellow school bus will cover with just one coat. We have buses that were painted three years ago and still look good. When you mix your paint, mix it no more than three parts paint to one part

86

thinner. If you keep the paint thick you will have fewer runs, although it will take a little longer to dry. If you use the three-to-one mixture, the bus will be dry in about 4 hours in 70 degree temperatures. Use ordinary newspaper to mask off the windows, lights, and mirrors. Be sure to tape all the gaskets around the windshield. Place the outer edge of the masking tape all around the outside edge of the gasket. Then put the newspaper in place, and press the free edge of the masking tape onto the newspaper to hold it in place. Use the same procedure for the lights and mirrors and reflectors. It helps to take the small reflectors off the bus, wipe down the place where the reflector was after the bus has been painted, then put the reflectors back on. Be sure to place rags or quilts over the tires when you paint to prevent the overspray from getting on the tires or rims.

I suggest you paint the buses a solid color. But if you do two-tone your buses, be sure you *do not* put masking tape on paint that is only two or three days old on the bus unless it has been baked on professionally. Masking tape on "green" paint will pull the paint off when you take the tape off. It is best not to leave masking tape even on old paint for more than two days. Especially in hot weather. We used masking tape to put Vacation Bible School signs on our buses one year. Two weeks later, when we pulled the signs off, we also pulled off a lot of paint. Some folks put signs on their automobiles, and the masking tape pulled the paint off their cars. So don't leave masking tape on the painted surfaces, especially in hot weather.

In preparing the buses for painting, we do not try to take out every dent. If you only intend to have two or three buses, you may want to put them in "showroom" condition. But when you have a fleet of buses, it is too expensive and time-consuming to hammer out every dent and scratch. When you are finally ready to paint your bus NEVER use lacquer! If you put lacquer over enamel, your bus will look like jelly because the lacquer will melt the enamel undercoat, and it will just run all over. Call some of the paint shops in your area to find what the charge is to paint a bus. Most will charge anywhere from $175.00 to $250.00. You can probably paint your own bus for $75.00 to $100.00. Buy your paint and thinner, then rent or borrow a spray gun and compressor. Always spray the buses. Do not brush the paint on. Brushed on paint always looks sloppy, and will not be a credit to your church.

Now let's talk about lettering the buses. To have a professional letter both sides of a bus will generally cost about $50.00. It may be there is someone in your church capable of doing a good lettering job. But be sure of their ability before letting them do it. It's a shame to have a bus with a nice paint job, only to have it ruined by a lettering job that looks like it came out of a first-grade grammar school class. I have seen lettering on buses that was unevenly spaced, that ran uphill and then downhill, that had fat letters and thin letters, and just about everything wrong that could make the bus look bad. If you're going to make the investment in a bus evangelism ministry, go ahead and have them properly lettered by a professional. You can order decals for your buses from Dice Decal Corporation, Box 165, Middlebrance, Ohio 44652. They will cost about $10.00 per decal, but they are professionally done and will look good when you put them on your buses. We have so many buses, that we had a professional come and teach us how to make our own decals. We can do both sides of about 8 buses for around $30.00 using a silk-screen process. The silk-screen or decal is as permanent as a paint job. They will not come off unless they are burned off or scraped off with a razor blade.

You may also want to use pictures on the outside of your buses. We have Bible scenes painted near the front of some of our buses. One has a picture of David and Goliath, another has a picture of Philip and the Ethiopian eunuch in his chariot, a third shows Elijah being carried up to heaven in a fiery chariot, while another shows Moses holding up the Ten Commandments. Still another shows Jesus carrying the cross. We do this because many children cannot associate with a number on the bus, but they will remember the picture. Many churches use secular pictures such as cartoon characters to identify their buses. There is nothing wrong with this. Choose whatever you feel is best for you. But please make it look good. Make it look professional, and be a credit to your church and to the Lord.

CHAPTER 20

PREVENTIVE MAINTENANCE

By Roland Steiner, Mechanic, Beth Haven Baptist Church

Preventive maintenance means just what it says. You are looking for something, or you are doing something that will prevent trouble later. How do you perform preventive maintenance? Before you ever get to Sunday morning, take the bus to the shop, grease it, check the oil in the rear axle and transmission. Check the tires and be sure they have the proper pressure. When I first came to the United States and worked in a service station, there was an older lady who came in every week for gas. When Fall came around, she would say, "Roland, I'd like you to change the air in my tires. Winter is coming on, and I want you to let the air out and put winter air in." Well, who am I to say "Don't do it?" So I changed the air! You won't want to go that far, but be sure to check the pressure regularly. Before sending the buses on the road, lift the hood and check the oil and water. A leaking or broken water hose will mean a break down. An engine that is blowing oil could get a few miles down the road and then lock up on you. Then you've got a $200.00 to $300.00 repair bill on your hands.

But what happens when, after you've checked everything, the bus goes out, the engine locks up, and it just won't go anymore? You're faced with the problem of how to get it fixed. One of the most important things to know is where to get the parts you need. Of course, you can go to the automotive dealers and buy what you need. But if you've got a blown engine, try a junk yard. The used truck parts places are plentiful, and you can save as much as $100.00 by buying from a reputable used parts dealer. A good dealer will give you some guarantee with the engine, so if it should go bad within the guarantee period, he will replace it without charge. I've never had an engine blow up on me that I have completely rebuilt myself, so I consider myself a top mechanic. But I must admit I have had some trouble with brakes once in a while. So go to the junk yards first. Then if you can't find what you need, go to the

89

automotive dealers. But be sure you know what you need, or have some competent advisors with you.

We try to keep our buses in good running condition. We run 30 buses every Sunday, and we have very few breakdowns. This is because we keep them in good condition during the week, and prevent many major problems from happening by getting to them as soon as something seems to be wrong.

Learn what parts can be interchanged. There are a lot of parts that can be interchanged, even though many of the dealers will tell you it can't be done. Many GMC parts will fit a Chevrolet, and Ford. An International transmission will fit in a Ford. You can get many of these major parts to fit almost anything. I have a book called "The Bible of Parts" which tells what parts can be interchanged with each other. It's really helpful to know what will fit into what when you go looking for used parts. Also it's a good idea to keep all your old parts, as you never know what you may need.

Get the best possible place to work on the buses that you can. It may be nice under the old shade tree during the summer, but it may be pretty cold in the winter. Try to find an abandoned station or an old barn that can be used for your maintenance work. And be sure to keep your work place clean. It's easy to get oil and grease all over the place, especially with volunteer help. You've got to make it clear that cleaning up is as much a part of the work as anything else. Try to find a group of men you can depend on to do a good job of work, but who will also clean up after the work is done.

One last thing—I make it a practice every morning, when I go down to the shop, to pray before I begin. Whatever you do, in all of your work, go to the Lord in prayer about it before you begin. He answers our prayers, and pours out the blessings. There have been many times, as I worked on some bus, that I was just at the end of my wits. I just couldn't figure out how to make it work. But I would get down on my knees, put my hands on that bus, and pray, "Now God, I'm taking my hands off this bus . . . it's yours!" And you know, so far He's always answered my prayer. He's never let me down.

PART V
FILL THE BUSES

CHAPTER 21
CONTESTS, AWARDS, GIFTS AND TREATS

We should have contests at least once a month. And don't be so concerned about what the method is, so long as your motive is right. Our motive is to glorify Christ in what we are doing. Our methods will change, but never the message. I suppose it used to be that everyone walked to church. Then they began to ride horses. Then they began to ride in buggies, and then in automobiles. Now we are using buses, and some are even using airplanes. You see, methods will change, but not the message. Look how much the airlines have changed in their methods. You no longer just get a ride from one place to another—you get soft chairs that recline, a stewardess to see to your comforts, pillows, soft drinks, magazines, snacks, full dinners, and even entertainment! Churches need to be watchful for more effective methods of reaching people, and adopt them as they prove practical. Jesus said, "Go ye into all the world and preach the gospel to every creature." So we are going out, and inviting people to come to the Lord's house. Luke 14 says, "Go out and invite them to a great supper." That was the use of food. We may use food, as with a picnic, but it's always to preach the same unchanging message of Christ. Here are some contests that can be used to stimulte competition between bus pastors. The bus pastor with the best record could win:

1. A new suit;
2. A steak dinner for his entire family;
3. A trip to a Bible conference or retreat;
4. A gift certificate to a good store;

5. A new Bible. We have often awarded the winning bus pastor a new Scofield Bible, the best that could be bought.

I recall one contest where the winning bus pastor had all his people gather around him while his flag was raised to the top of a flagpole, while the other bus teams saluted. It is rewarding to the winner, and humbling to the losers, and stimulates some good competition. Sometimes we will have a contest with the wife of the winning bus pastor receiving some nice award. At Christmas we may have a contest for the best-decorated bus. And the bus riders can be really inventive to make the buses look extra-nice. There will be cards hanging from the ceiling, frost on the windows, a manger scene up in the front, garlands criss-crossing the interior. One bus had a stocking hanging at each seat for each child who came. Our buses look beautiful on Christmas Sunday morning, and all our deacons must come early, before the buses go out on the road, and vote for the top three buses. The three top winners receive a nice gift.

Another contest is where one bus challenges another to a tug-of-war on a particular Sunday. The bus team will take special brochures when they visit on Saturday. It may say something like: "The punny runts of bus number one have challenged us Mighty Giants of bus number ten to a tug-of-war! Boys and girls, Moms and Dads, are we going to let bus number one beat us in a tug-of-war? No, we're not! And if we beat them, we win the contest. If we out-pull them on the rope, we go home; and eat ice cream, while they go home sucking their thumbs! Be sure to be on the bus (date) for the greatest tug-of-war!" This has worked greatly for us. It has helped to increase our attendance during months when attendance would normally be low. One year the bus workers challenged the Sunday school workers to a contest to see who could make the most personal contacts. The Sunday school workers felt quite confident, since there were 280 of them, against only 18 bus pastors. But the bus pastors won by more than 3,000 contacts on that weekend. But there were over 12,000 contacts turned in between those bus pastors and the Sunday school workers, and we all benefitted. We had one of the greatest services in the church. We had our largest Sunday school attendance ever on that Sunday, simply because of a contest between our people to see who could invite the most. We have had that contest twice since then, and the bus pastors have won 2 out of 3 times. Contests will keep people motivated and moving for the Lord.

Awards, (or rewards) are great in getting people to come to church. On the Fourth of July we will give each child a small flag. The flag will cost about a penny each. The Sunday school lesson will be on "Blessed is the nation whose Lord is God." We may award a Bible to the one who brings the most new people, or for the most new riders on a bus.

We have an effective radio ministry at our church, and each year we have radio Sunday. We may give transistor radios as awards. During the month of March, we have Kite Sunday, and all the boys and girls receive a kite and a ball of string. There may be some fad going around, like yo-yo's, or sun glasses. At Christmas we give them an apple or an orange or a bag of candy. We may take them on a trip to a nice place. We want to keep our people excited about God's work, so will reward them for coming to church, or for faithful attendance, or for helping in some way.

We often give treats to the boys and girls who come. We may have a popcorn treat. On Popcorn Sunday, all the boys and girls receive a bag of popcorn on the way home. Sometimes we have Breakfast On The Bus, and give them hot chocolate and donuts. If you do this, be sure to fill the cups only half-full to avoid spills. Many of the parents would not get up to fix breakfast for their children, and would not let the children come if we did not give them something to eat. In the summertime, we may stop for a watermelon feast. This is a lot of fun, and also provides a good time for fellowship and for people to get to know each other better. It's a real good time where people feel not only that we want them in church, but that we love them, and want to have fun with them, too. Every Sunday each bus pastor gets a box of suckers to give out on the way home from church. We may have a picnic for the boys and girls. We tell them to bring a sack lunch on a particular day, and we stop by the park on the way home. We play games with them, but usually have different games for the boy and the girls. In the wintertime, we may use our fellowship hall to show them a Christmas movie, and they can have a sandwich and Coke. We love our boys and girls, and want to give them treats as much as possible to show them how we feel about them.

CHAPTER 22
SUPPLIERS OF
PROMOTIONAL MATERIALS

If you are not able to locate promotional items in your town, write to the following for catalogues. We have used materials from most of these, and have been satisfied.

1. Adver-tek, P. O. Box 678, Lexington, Ky.

2. Wright Industries, 139 Loretta Ave. Dayton, Ohio

3. Jimmie Conti and Son, 1757 Frankfort Ave. Louisville, Ky 40206

4. Hewig and Marvic Advertisers, 861 Manhattan Ave. Brooklyn, N.Y. 11222

5. Magnaphonics, 130 E. National Rd. Vandalia, Ohio 45377

6. Cruden Mfg. Co. Box 508, St. Louis, Mo. 63166

7. R. K. Walker Flag Co. Rear 313 Esplande Ave. Louisville, Ky. 40214

8. Ministry of Ideas, Box 24666, Dallas, Texas

9. Miracle Traffic Builders, 861 Manhattan Avenue, Brooklyn, N.Y. 11222

10. Mapac Company, Bellmore, N.Y. 11710

11. Ross Company, Liberty, N.Y. 12854

12. CBE Supply, P. O. Box 90361, Nashville, Tenn. 37209

13. Beth Haven Baptist Church, 5515 Johnsontown Road, Louisville, Ky. 40272

14. Bring Them In magazine, Box 90008, Nashville, Tenn. 37209

CHAPTER 23

AN EXAMPLE OF
THE FIRST EIGHT WEEKS

By William A. Powell
Atlanta, Georgia

During the spring I assisted First Baptist Church, Atlanta, to launch their Church Bus Evangelism ministry. The following is a report I prepared for the Pastor, Dr. Charles F. Stanley, for the first eight weeks.

We experienced the usual delays and problems in recruiting and training workers; raising the money to purchase buses; finding good buses to purchase; getting them renovated and lettered; handling all the people who came; launching the Graded Church Services properly; and the adjustments that are needed when the attendance pattern is suddenly reversed from a declining trend to a rapid growth pattern. But in spite of all the problems, the blessings of God were upon the faithful labors of the dedicated workers. The Pastor and the Youth Director, Mrs. Wright Gellerstedt, gave untiring efforts and leadership in this effort.

The average Sunday school attendance was about 1,800 per week about ten years ago. Since that time, there had been a decline in attendance that averaged about 80 per year for the past 10 years. The Sunday school attendance for the year prior to March 1972 was about 1,000 per week. The last Sunday I was with them was May 14, and their Sunday school attendance was 1,750 on that day.

They baptized 38 people during 1970, and 46 during 1971. They baptized 98 during the month of May, 1972—more than they baptized during the entire two previous years!

There was a spirit of revival, of interest, enthusiasm, and dedication resulting from the moving of God's Spirit in the church, and the greatly increased attendance and baptisms.

This report is included as a matter of information, not as a

model, or in any sense of boasting. Other churches have accomplished greater increases in attendance and baptisms, but
these bus captains were able to achieve a high average number
of riders per bus route, and this contributed largely to the
spiritual results.

1972 DATE	Sundays To Use the Buses	Bus Routes	TOTAL NUMBER OF Bus Riders	FIRST TIME BUS RIDERS This Sunday	Since Starting	Average Number of Bus Riders Per Bus Route
3-12	1	2	59	31	31	30
3-19	2	2	89	31	62	45
3-26	3	4	157	65	127	39
4-2*	4	4	105	22	149	26
4-9	5	4	231	98	247	58
4-16	6	4	262	66	313	65
4-23	7	4	357	76	389	89
4-30**	8	5	421	124	513	84

*Easter
**Time change Sunday

CHAPTER 24
STATISTICS ON BUS EVANGELISM

By Michael Claunch, Shawnee Oklahoma

The following is a report of a questionnaire survey on bus outreach ministry. Out of fifty questionnaires that were sent to churches across the country, twenty-six were returned. Eighteen of the twenty-six had a currently operating bus outreach ministry, and completed the majority of the questions asked. Therefore this summary is based on the answers received on the eighteen questionnaires returned by churches from Alaska to Florida.

The responding churches ranged from under 500 in membership to over 2,000, with half the churches having over 1750 members, and an average attendance of over 750. No rural churches reported, and only three churches were in cities of less than 50,000. Most were in cities of 50,000 or more population, and located in the suburbs. A few downtown churches in the large cities also responded. Most of the bus ministries examined were in their first year of operation, although one church had been using buses in outreach for thirty-one years. A large majority began the bus ministry with only one or two buses, and the average number of buses, as of January, 1972 was seven per church. The average budget allotments was $13,050. Churches were split equally on renting or buying buses, but those who bought generally bought old buses for around $1,100 each. Rental prices averaged about $21 per run per bus. Most churches owning buses maintain them with professional mechanics, although minor repairs are done by volunteer help. Maintenance costs averaged around $400 per year. Most bus-owning churches carried 100/300 liability insurance for protection. All ran their buses Sunday mornings, and about one-third ran on Sunday night also. Only one-sixth ran any of their buses on Wednesday night.

Many churches considered proximity to church, and the results of a church census to select their bus routes. A few also considered the socio-economic status of the neighborhood, and several examined the population density. Almost all of the routes were less than 10 miles in length, although one church ran a route sixty miles long. Sixty per cent of the churches had a director of bus outreach, and all use bus pastors (captains, missionaries) with assistants who help in visitation and management of the bus.

Saturday canvass and visitation of referrals made by members is used by most churches to find bus riders. The initial contact with the rider is always made by a personal visit, and regular riders are contacted weekly by a visit, or sometimes by phone. Sixty-two per cent of the riders are between first and sixth grades. Younger children, juniors and senior high school students account for most of the other riders. Adults made up about 8% of those riding the buses. Most buses are transporting Caucasian riders almost exclusively. Only small numbers of other ethnic groups are riding. Eighty per cent of people riding the buses are reported to be of middle income families, or below. The average number of riders per bus is 33.

A number of churches have not adjusted Sunday morning activities because of their bus ministry, but most of the churches having a large ministry have added children's worship services. A few use an orientation program, and two have a separate Sunday school for bus children. Curriculum materials from the Sunday School Board, and Child Evangelism Fellowship are the most popular being used. The average teacher/pupil ratio reported was 1/7. Over half the churches use some type of promotional methods including rewards for coming, rewards for bringing friends, parties, trips, etc. The average annual cost of this promotion was $600.

On the bus, singing is the primary activity used with Bible games running second. Bible reading and stories are used by a few. Suggestions for maintaining discipline on the bus included limiting participation in extra activities, preventing the rider, from coming for a certain number of Sundays, and taking the child home by car.

Almost all of the pitfalls reported were centered around not having enough people participating in the various parts of the program, particularly visitation and teaching. Connected with this was lack of training of those who do serve.

Every church with a working bus outreach ministry showed gains in the Sunday morning activities membership and attendance. Baptisms increased in many churches. Only budget receipts failed to show a marked increase as a result of the ministry.

PART VI
PREPARING FOR THE FIRST SUNDAY

CHAPTER 25
THE PASTOR

1. Plan the launching of your C.B.E. (Church Bus Evangelism) ministry in light of the fact it can be the best way known for evangelizing your area. Many churches have seen dramatic increases in attendance and baptisms (double, triple, etc.) within a few months (or weeks).

2. Recognize that the way you launch your C.B.E. ministry will have a major bearing upon its success or failure. Note my outline "Some Things That Can Contribute To Failure in the C.B.E. Ministry."

3. Attend one or two of the full two day C.B.E. clinics. The Evangelism Division of the Home Mission Board is helping conduct these clinics throughout the nation.

4. Study all available books and material.

5. There are some other recent outlines I have used that will be helpful:

    a. Guidelines to Double the Attendance, Triple the Baptisms, and Quadruple the Interest and Enthusiasm

    b. Steps To Take in Beginning An Effective Church Bus Evangelism Ministry

    c. All of the outlines under the heading of "Preparing for the First Saturday"

        1). The C.B.E. Director

        2). The Bus Captain

        3). The Bus Driver

        4). The Sunday School Director

        5). The Music Director

        6). The Teenage Crusader

7). The Martha Club President
' 8). The Leader of the Graded Church Services
d. Some Essentials for the Most Effective Church Bus
   Evangelism Ministry.

6. Probably your most valuable contribution will be in the recruiting and training of workers, and in providing proper support to the workers, and giving careful oversight to the entire project. You will not have time to get tied up in the details of the various things that should be delegated to others such as buying and renovating buses, and securing supplies, materials, and so on.

7. Give all the guidance, support, and encouragement you can to the various people involved in successfully launching this project.

8. Go and observe some other churches who are successfully engaged in an aggressive C.B.E. ministry. Visit the churches that are averaging at least 40 or 50 or more per bus and are gradually adding more buses.

9. It will be very profitable for you to visit with two to four of these churches before you have been in the C.B.E. ministry six months. You can obtain some good ideas and observe some weak points to avoid in each church you visit.

10. This will probably involve one or more out of town trips. But the results from these study trips will repay the expense and inconveniences. On the out of town trips it probably is best to arrive in the city in adequate time to get a good night's sleep Friday night.

11. Be at the church Saturday morning when they begin the Bus Captains' meeting. Go out visiting with them all day Saturday. Meet with them Saturday night for their prayer time. Ride one of the buses Sunday morning as they pick up riders. Observe how they get all the children into their proper places for Sunday School. Observe their various age groups of the Graded Church Services. Note how they get them all back on the buses. Ride one of the buses as they take them home. Ride on a bus that has some special activity planned for that Sunday afternoon if possible.

12. It is usually quite wise to get some of the deacons active in the C.B.E. ministry in the beginning. Some prayer meetings with

the deacons praying specifically for laborers for the harvest (as Jesus commanded) will be helpful. Pray earnestly that God will warm the hearts of the people so that they will be willing to give their Saturdays for helping to evangelize the community. God answers prayer. James said that you have not because you ask not. Pray that some of the deacons will be willing to be Bus Captains.

13. Your deacons should spend a lot of time with you in prayer for the workers and for God's guidance and blessings. There may even be some deacons who are reluctant to give up the things they are doing on Saturdays to help in this. Pray that each of the deacons will be responsive to the call of God as God wants them to respond. Pray that the deacons will set the proper example for the other church members.

14. Imagine the outcome of a serious battle when the generals are not actively involved. Battles are lost if the generals send the soldiers to war while they stay home and wish them well.

15. Expect the devil to become quite active in slowing down, or crippling, or preventing this project. He will try to create circumstances, cause unexpected problems, and influence some key people within your community and within your church to endanger and jeopardize the success of this project. And he has been quite successful in this on many occasions.

16. But you are waging battle against the devil from the vantage point of strength and victory. We are more than conquerors through Him. And greater is He that is in you than he that is in the world.

17. Do not permit the ordinary delay tactics that the devil usually causes to delay the launching beyond a reasonable date.

18. Do not become discouraged if every detail cannot be properly handled prior to the first Saturday. Do the best you can to get as many of the things taken care of as possible. I know of no church that has had an "ideal" launching. Battles are never won under ideal conditions. Make all preparations possible and when the battle is launched, give it the best you have. Make whatever adjustments, changes, and improvisions necessary for success. Strive for the ideal but do the best you can with what you have. There is something exciting about winning a major battle.

CHAPTER 26
THE BUS DIRECTOR

1. Attend at least one or two of the full two day C.B.E. clinics, sponsored by Beth Haven Baptist Church or Total Evangelistic Concepts.

2. Read all available material about the C.B.E. ministry. A bibliography is attached that includes most of the books.

3. Visit other churches that are successfully engaged in an aggressive C.B.E. ministry, such as Beth Haven Baptist Church, 5515 Johnsontown Road, Louisville, Ky.

4. If you have not already served successfully as a bus captain, then plan to serve as one of the first bus captains. Serve until you have built a route from zero to average at least 50 riders per week for one month or more.

5. After you have built a route to average at least 50 riders per week for a month, it may be wise to discontinue serving as a bus captain. This will give you time to serve more effectively as the C.B.E. Director. But it is usually assumed that no man can serve successfully as a C.B.E. Director until he has built a route from zero to average 50 or more riders per week for at least one month.

6. One of the important things the C.B.E. Director does when he does not have his own route is to help establish new routes. Also he helps revive weak routes. He also is involved in training new bus workers.

7. Adjust your personal schedule so as to be available all day for the first few Saturdays.

8. Plan to be at the church by 8:00 or 8:15 each Saturday morning.

9. Have a capable and responsible team committed for each bus route. Make sure each captain knows the exact boundaries of the area for his route.

10. Seek the best captains possible. Remember that availability, dependability, and dedication are the most important factors.

11. Make sure there is a reliable co-captain for each bus route.

12. Make sure that there is a safe and competent driver for each bus.

13. Make sure there are two teenage crusaders for each bus route.

14. See that each team has a reasonable amount of training and instructions.

15. Make sure that each worker has studied the material pertinent to his responsibility.

16. See that each team has gone and observed some other successful teams. This could be other teams in your church but it would be better if it were with teams in other nearby churches.

17. It may require an extra special effort and expenses for your teams to go and observe some other teams. But this will pay rich dividends—and especially if they go and observe some teams that have considerable successful experience.

18. Make sure that the teenage crusaders are properly assigned to the various bus teams. Know which teenager is responsible for the program on each bus.

19. Conduct some training sessions for the bus driver. When you have several drivers it is possible that some one from the public school system or the state highway department would help train your bus drivers.

20. Some helpful material is available from General Motors for training the bus drivers. Some of it is free and some costs. Write them at:

GMC Truck and Coach Division
660 South Boulevard, East
Pontiac, Mich. 48053

21. Make sure that your leaders of the Graded Church Services have adequate materials and program helps and that they have adequate training.

22. Make sure your leaders of the Graded Church Services are prepared for the influx of children from each bus route established.

23. Have a definite understanding as to what time your leaders of the Graded Church Services will dismiss the children. Some dismiss at a set time (e.g. 12:00). But most churches wait

and dismiss them about the same time that the "big church" in the auditorium dismisses, regardless of when that is.

24. Arrange for some one to keep the nursery each Saturday from 8:30 until 5:00.

25. Do not overload your bus workers with extra work unless they volunteer for it. The responsibility of the bus workers is to enlist riders, bring them to church, get them in the proper places, and take them back home after church is over.

26. No bus worker is expected to help with the children during Sunday School or during the worship hour just because they are bus workers. Some bus workers will do double duty and help with the riders during Sunday School and/or the worship hour. Their responsibility as a bus worker concludes when they get all the riders in the proper places. And it begins again when they are dismissed for boarding the buses. However, their responsibility as Christians and church members will motivate some of the bus workers to help with the riders in the teaching, training, and worship programs.

27. Your bus workers will do more to help evangelize your area than any other group in the church. They will cause a greater increase in attendance and baptisms than any other group in the church. They will do more to transform your church into a growing, aggressive, thriving, New Testament church than anything that has ever happened to your church. All of these will result if you see that they receive the proper training, adequate support, the right motivation, and proper supervision. Remember that you have a "tiger by the tail" that can completely revolutionize the average church. Love your bus workers, support them, encourage them, provide them the materials they need, provide them with adequate training, and pray earnestly and constantly for them and with them.

28. Arrange for the Supervisor of Bus Maintenance to be at the church each Sunday morning by the time the first driver arrives. He should remain at the church until all the buses have left to take the riders back home. It may be wise for him to remain there until all the buses have returned to the church and been properly parked.

29. Do not permit the Bus Captains to become involved in

maintaining and servicing the buses. This will detract from the time they have available to do their work.

30. Have the names and phone numbers of some substitute bus drivers.

31. Consult very carefully with the Pastor as to the areas for each route.

32. Careful attention must be devoted to the selection of the areas for the bus routes. As a rule it is best to establish the routes near the church building. They should be established in areas where there is a large number of children or a large number of retired people.

33. Make sure that there is a bus that has been renovated, painted, lettered, and ready to go for each route.

34. Arrange a room for keeping bus supplies, records, promotional items, etc. This room must be kept locked. It is good if this room is large enough for the bus workers to have their meetings.

35. Have an adequate quantity of name badges printed. Probably the most economical method is to have a metal plate made so they can be printed on the church offset press. (If the church does not own an offset, perhaps arrangements can be made with some church that does have one to print them. Or hire the print shop to print them). They should be printed on fairly heavy paper—something about as heavy as index cards—90 lb. to 120 lb. Most churches prefer printing them on colored stock—green, blue, yellow, etc. Print the name, address, and phone number on them. Leave adequate space for the bus workers to write their names on them. Note the sheet showing how our church did it. The main cost is having the metal plate made and purchasing the 90 lb. colored paper.

36. The usual design of these name badge inserts is:

WOODLAWN BAPTIST CHURCH
1772 Columbia Drive
Decatur, Georgia
Telephone 289-2949
"Please ride our bus to church Sunday"

37. About 8 or 10 of these can be run on a single 8½x11" sheet. *Care must be exercised when cutting the sheet into individual name badges.* Cut them for an exact fit in the badge holders.

38. Obtain an adequate quantity of the plastic name badge holders. There are three different types. One type has a lower portion for inserting in the pocket. Another type has a safety pin for attaching to the clothing. The third type has a bulldog clip on it for clipping to collars, lapels, or other portions of clothing. It is important to obtain some of all three types. All three types will need to hold the same size name badge. The most popular size seems to be for name card size 2¼x3½.

39. Have a supply of felt pins for the workers to use in putting their names on the name badge inserts.

40. Obtain an adequate supply of the Prospective Bus Rider's cards. (Probably about 500 per route).

41. Order a supply of the "Bus Captain's Weekly Report Cards." About 100 per route.

42. Obtain an adequate quantity of the "Weekly Report of the C.B.E. Director." About two or three pads. They usually come in pads of 100.

43. Obtain an adequate supply of the "Bus Driver's Monthly Report" cards. About 25 per bus route.

44. Obtain a looseleaf notebook for each captain. The kind I like best are those with a 1" capacity to contain 5"x8" sheets with 16 rings. It seems best to have the 16 rings because the sheets will not tear out as easily as if there are only 3 rings. These notebooks receive a lot of (rough) treatment each Saturday and Sunday.

45. The 5x8 forms with 16 holes and the matching notebooks with 6 rings are available from C.B.E. Supply at P.O. Box 90361, Nashville, Tennessee 37209. The 3½x6 forms with 6 holes and the matching pocket size 6 ring notebooks are also available from the C.B.E. Supply.

46. These are also available for the 5x8 size sheets with 3 rings.

47. There are some 5x8 forms available with 3 holes from the Baptist Book Stores.

48. Also, there are pocket size notebooks with 6 rings available for 3½x6 sheets. Many captains prefer these because they can carry them in the pocket or purse. However these only have a ½" capacity. This means the captain that has a large route may

need two or more of these notebooks to contain all his riders. Even so many captains will prefer the pocket size notebook.

49. Order an adequate number of the "Bus Captain's Permanent Records" for each captain. (Probably about 200 for each route). These enable you to list all riders in any one family on the same sheet. This gives one sheet in the book for each family rather than one sheet for each rider. It saves valuable time for the captains when all riders in any one family are included on the same sheet. It is a little more complicated and requires a little more time when you have one separate sheet for each rider. It saves time when enrolling new riders and in the regular weekly records. This is especially true when there are several children in a family.

50. Put the captain's name and route number on his notebook. The gummed embossed tape labels are good for this.

51. Have an adequate number of brochures or leaflets prepared. (Probably about 500 for each route). The workers use these quite widely in the Saturday visitation. One is left in the home of every prospective rider and at every house where no one is at home.

52. These brochures or leaflets usually come in about four different types. One is folding type with pictures and printing designed to appeal to adults. These are usually fairly expensive. Another type is the mimeographed folder with free hand art work and lettering designed to appeal to children. These are usually inexpensive. Another type is the 5½"x8½" flat mimeographed sheet. Another is the 8½"x11" flat mimeographed sheet. You may order some or have some printed.

53. These should list the name, address, and telephone number of the church; the name and telephone number of the pastor; and the name and telephone number of the bus captain. This local information can be applied by means of rubber stamps on the forms you purchase. Space should be left for the pick-up time and return time to be written in by the bus worker.

54. Obtain a 1½" rubber stamp with the church information on it. This is to be used in stamping literature that is distributed that does not have this information printed on it. Four lines is usually best, as follows:

NAME BAPTIST CHURCH
Street Address
City, State, Zip

NAME OF PASTOR

55. Have a 1½″ rubber stamp made for each captain. The way I like to have them made:

CAPTAIN WILLIAM A. POWELL
Church Bus Captain
Home Phone 289-8799
Church Phone 289-2949

56. Order an adequate supply of the magic cards for the workers who desire to use them in enlisting new riders. (CBE Supply, P.O. Box 90361, Nashville, Tenn.)

57. Secure a candy bag for each captain that desires one. Most captains prefer the shaving kit bag with a zipper on it.

58. Obtain an adequate supply of candy and bubblegum for the workers who want to give it out to the children.

59. Obtain a broom and waste can for each bus. Mark each one with the number of the bus on it. Mark them in such a way that it will stay.

60. Check with the Martha Club President to insure that all plans are in order for breakfast at 8:45 Saturday.

61. Arrange for coffee and rolls to be at the church at 7:30 each Sunday morning.

62. Have a definite understanding as to where the buses will unload and where they will be parked during Sunday School and church.

63. Have a definite understanding with Sunday School Director and bus workers as to where all new riders go upon arrival at church and the procedures for getting them all properly registered.

64. Check with the Sunday School Director to insure that he is all set.

65. One good promotional idea is to present each captain with a nice gift on his first Sunday. This presentation is made public. The label states that the gift is to be opened on the Sunday he brings in 50 or more riders. This provides some incentive to build the route quickly.

66. Consult with each bus team about providing some special activity for their riders one Sunday during the first month. This party takes place after church on the way home.

67. Consult with your Bus Captains in establishing challenging and realistic goals.

68. Remember that there is nothing being done in any community or church that the devil hates more than a strong concerted effort to evangelize the lost. He will put forth every possible effort to delay, defeat, slow down the work, discourage the workers, and hinder this effort. Remember that he is in position to control circumstances and to influence many good people in the community and in the church.

69. Paul says, "Don't let others spoil your faith and joy with their philosophies, their wrong and shallow answers built on men's thoughts and ideas, instead of on what Christ has said." Colossians 2:8 Living Bible.

70. But we engage in this spiritual battle from a standpoint of strength and victory. John reminds us that "greater is He that is in you than he that is in the world." I John 4:4KJV.

71. Please do not delay launching the C.B.E. ministry until you have everything in perfect order. Set your launch date at a reasonable time and do everything possible to be as nearly ready as possible. Then blast off on the launch date. Remember that very few battles are won under ideal circumstances.

72. "I will do the best I can with what I have where I am for Jesus' sake today and try to be ready to do His will for me tomorrow."

73. Pray as if everything depended upon God and work as if everything depended upon you.

CHAPTER 27
THE BUS CAPTAIN

1. Decide what type of a Bus Captain you are going to be. The happy, enthused, and most successful Bus Captain are those who average *five hours or more* in visitation each Saturday and average 50 or more riders each week and see many people accept Christ.

2. The happiest Bus Captains are those who work the hardest, have the biggest loads, and see the most people saved. Many of these Bus Captains are responsible for more people being saved each year than many preachers are.

3. Most Bus Captains who do not schedule a specific number of hours each week for visitation (and then stick to that schedule religiously) will wind up visiting only an hour or so each Saturday, and bringing in only 15-25 riders each week, and seeing only a small number of people saved. Many of these Captains get discouraged easily and quit.

4. The average Captain with a reasonable amount of training and experience should average about 10 riders each Sunday for each hour he averages in visitation each week. The Captain that averages five hours visitation each week should average about 50 riders.

5. Decide how much of your Saturdays you are willing to give up for Christ and seeing people saved. This may be compared with buying stock in a growing company—how much are you really willing to invest in a sure thing??

6. Set your personal goals high. Plan to make a major contribution to the efforts of your church to evangelize the area. Give it your best.

7. Put forth a special effort to have a large number of riders the first Sunday.

8. Begin thinking of the time when you will go over the 100 mark in your riders. Let me know when you reach the 100 mark so you can be included in the "Bus Captains' Hall of Fame."

9. There is a lot involved and many details to take care of in establishing a good bus route. It is a challenging and time consuming project for the first several weeks. But as the weeks go by

and the route is established fairly well, the Bus Captain learns to "ride the tide and roll with punches." It becomes an enjoyable and rewarding experience, paying rich dividends on the investment.

10. Plan after the first weekend to visit each regular rider, each absentee, and each known prospect each Saturday. Plan to use as much time as possible each Saturday enlisting new riders.

11. Plan minimum personal social involvements on Friday nights and Saturday nights for the first few weeks.

12. Spend from two to five Saturdays visiting with other *successful* Bus Captains. It is best to visit with at least two or three different Captains so as to observe strong points and weak points of each one. Visit with Captains who will average at least 40 or more riders per week. It is best to visit with Captains who average 60-75 or more riders each week.

13. Ride with some other Captains on two or three Sundays as they pick up the riders and then as they take them back home.

14. Become familiar with the best ways of enlisting riders. The best way is to find the children out playing, enlist them, and then go see their parents. The magic cards, the bumble bee, and other such items are very valuable in this approach. The next best way is getting the children to go with you to enlist their friends. The third best way is going from house to house knocking on doors. Other methods such as putting up posters, distributing leaflets, telephoning, mailing announcements, advertising on radio, T.V., newspaper, etc., have very little value so far as enlisting children to ride the bus.

15. Confer with the C.B.E. Director about the selection of the area for your route. Consideration is given to any area for which the Captain feels a special burden. The proper selection of the area for your route is very important. Seek God's will in this matter.

16. Know the exact boundaries of your assigned area. This will insure no overlap with other captains in your church.

17. Become familiar with the assigned area.

18. Visualize the approximate route your bus will follow within the assigned area.

19. Plan the general area of your first pick-up and your last

pick-up. The first stop is usually the most distant rider and the last stop is the nearest rider.

20. Plan the approximate pick-up time for the first step. This should usually be about one hour before Sunday School begins.

21. Plan your schedule so as *to be able* to return to the church about 20 to 30 minutes before Sunday School begins on the first Sunday or so.

22. Do *not* return to church until about 10 minutes before Sunday School begins. Plan for an excess of 15 to 20 minutes. Use this excess time by driving slowly, and going down streets unnecessarily.

23. This "excess time" the first few Sundays will provide additional time as the number of riders increase. This will prevent the necessity of moving back the time of your first stop each Sunday. It is also good advertising for your bus route in your area. It also gives you a little more time to get acquainted with your riders and for them to get acquainted with the system.

24. Have the name and telephone number of your Co-captain.

25. Have the name and telephone number of your driver.

26. Have the names and telephone numbers of your Teenage Crusaders. Know which one will lead the program on your bus each Sunday as the children are brought to church and taken home.

27. Make sure the driver has the bus clean and ready to go. A broom and waste can must be on each bus. A supply of cloths for wiping the seats each Sunday morning will be necessary. Note the other items listed for the driver.

28. Plan to use all day Saturday, at least on the first few Saturdays.

29. Find out who will help you with the visitation on the first Saturday. See that they receive some type of experience or training if at all possible before the first Saturday.

30. Plan the blocks or areas for your helpers to work in on their first Saturday.

31. Obtain an adequate quantity of:
    a. Brochures to leave in the homes.
    b. Prospective Bus Rider cards.
    c. A Bus Captain's notebook.

  d. Sheets (forms) for the Bus Captain's notebook.

  e. Bus Captain's Weekly Report cards.

32. Obtain a rubber stamp for all of the hand-out literature. Here is the way I like the stamp made:

CAPTAIN WILLIAM A. POWELL
Church Bus Captain
Home Phone 289-8799
Church Phone 289-2949

33. Arrange to be on time for the meeting of the bus workers each Saturday morning. *Do not plan to go back home until your visitation is completed Saturday afternoon.* You and your workers can get a quick sandwich for lunch at a drive-in and keep going. Going home for lunch is usually a serious handicap for Bus Captains. Don't start it.

34. Make sure your name label is on your bus Captain's notebook.

35. Have a name badge for each person on your team. The plastic badges for inserting name cards are better than the kind that sticks to the coat or shirt.

36. Have a definite understanding as to the time and place your team meets each Sunday morning.

37. Have a definite understanding as to where to unload the children upon arrival at the church—and where the bus is to be parked during the morning services.

38. Have a definite understanding as to where each child will go upon arrival at the church. Some of them may go to an orientation Sunday School class for unchurched children and others may go to their regular classes. Oftentimes you will have children going to a number of different rooms and this necessitates several of your workers guiding them to their proper rooms.

39. Have an understanding as to the time the children are dismissed. In some churches they are automatically dismissed at a set time (e.g. 12:00 o'clock). But in most churches they are dismissed about the same time as the "big church" is dismissed in the auditorium.

40. Arrange to be on your bus as the children are dismissed and begin boarding.

41. If you have specific responsibilities during Sunday School, request that you be relieved of them for the first few Sundays because of your bus route.

42. Your responsibility as a Bus Captain terminates when you get all the children to their proper rooms. It begins again when the children are dismissed for boarding the buses.

43. As a Bus Captain you are not responsible for the riders during Sunday School and church. However, you are free to help during Sunday School and church if you so desire. And many Bus Captains do—but this is not a part of their responsibility as a Bus Captain.

44. Do not become involved with the servicing, maintenance, and operation of the bus. Leave that all to your driver.

45. Your team members will turn in to you all the Prospective Bus Rider cards they have filled out when they finish their visitation for the day. Discuss each card with the workers as they hand them to you. Make any pertinent note on these cards when they turn them in to you.

46. After your workers have turned in their Prospective Bus Rider cards, go visit each person who said they might ride your bus the next day. Get acquainted with them and where they live. Make sure they understand the approximate pick-up time. Tell them you will phone them Sunday morning to inform them the exact pick-up time. Discuss any other pertinent matters with them.

47. Make out one sheet for each family that you will probably have a rider on your bus tomorrow and put it in your notebook.

48. Place these sheets in your notebook in the order of pick-up. The first sheet in your book will be your first stop. The last sheet will be your last stop.

49. After you have arranged the sheets in the pick-up order, drive your car (or bus) throughout the entire route. Note each house or apartment where you will be stopping.

50. Make any additional follow-up telephone calls that you or your workers feel would be appropriate late Saturday afternoon or night.

51. Arrange for all of your family to ride the bus with you picking up children the first few Sunday mornings if feasible.

52. Find out the amount of money in the budget each month for promotions and activities for your route.

53. Secure a candy bag if you desire one. Many captains like to use a shaving kit bag like those men use in traveling. Keep it filled with an assortment of candy and bubblegum.

54. Plan a special activity for your riders about the third or fourth Sunday. Then plan to have some special activities about every month. These socials should always be after church Sunday afternoon—never on Saturday. Picnic, trip to zoo, trip to the country, trip to the city, trip to the airport with airplane rides for those who brought 3 visitors, pony rides, play ball, etc. The Co-captain usually plans these activities and helps a great deal with them. Of course the Teenage Crusaders are of vital importance in these activities.

55. Pray very sincerely that God will guide you and bless the work of your team.

CHAPTER 28
THE BUS DRIVER

1. Make sure your bus is clean. This usually requires extra special efforts in preparation for the first Sunday.

2. Make sure that you have a broom and a waste can for your bus. The number of your bus needs to be put on these in such a way that it will stay.

3. GIVE SPECIAL ATTENTION TO SAFETY.

4. Drive your bus around in the community until you are familiar with it. It will be very helpful for you to take it home with you and drive it several times during the week before the first Sunday.

5. Make sure that you are familiar enough with your bus so as to operate it safely.

6. Make sure your bus is in a safe operating condition.

7. Make note of any special needs for maintenance and discuss these with the Supervisor of Bus Maintenance.

8. Make sure that the rear door is securely fastened so that some person does not open it accidentally.

9. Make sure the rear door will operate easily in case of an emergency.

10. Make sure that the horn, brakes, and windshield wiper operates satisfactorily.

11. Adjust all mirrors so that an adequate view can be maintained on both sides and the rear of the bus.

12. If your bus has been recently painted, be careful about washing it with strong detergent, or taping anything to it, or removing any tape that has been applied.

13. Make sure the inspection sticker is current if the state law requires one.

14. Make sure there is a current license plate on the bus.

15. Have some cloths available for wiping the seats each Sunday morning before leaving.

16. Secure some type of small tool box for some simple basic

tools to carry on the bus each Sunday. You should keep these in your car when you are not driving the bus.

17. Know where the jumper cables are kept in case your battery is low.

18. Have the name and phone number of your Bus Captain.

19. Have a definite understanding with your Bus Captain as to the time to leave on Sunday morning.

20. Know the name and phone number of one or more substitute drivers you can call in case of emergency. It is *always* the driver's job to arrange for a substitute driver any time he cannot drive. It is *never* the Bus Captain's responsibility.

21. Attend all special training sessions held for the Bus Drivers.

22. Attend any other special meetings as requested by your Bus Captain or the C.B.E. Director.

23. You will probably need to attend the bus workers' meeting on the first Saturday morning. This is usually a breakfast meeting at 8:45.

24. Study carefully the job description and instructions for the Bus Driver.

25. Have a definite understanding about purchasing fuel and servicing for the bus. Each driver is usually furnished a credit card that he keeps and charges all fuel and services for his bus.

26. DO NOT EVER BACK THE BUS WITHOUT SOME RESPONSIBLE PERSON LOOKING IN THE AREA YOU WILL BE BACKING.

27. Crank the bus and drive it some on the first Saturday.

28. Arrange with your Bus Captain to drive the route late Saturday afternoon to become familiar with it.

29. Make sure your bus is warm and ready to go on time Sunday morning.

30. Have a supply of the "Bus Driver's Monthly Report Cards."

31. Assume the attitude that this is *my* bus that *my* church gave *me* to use in serving *my* Lord.

32. Plan to maintain and drive the bus in light of this attitude.

33. Dedicate yourself to being the best and most effective Bus Driver possible.

34. Ask God to save many people who ride your bus. And that the parents and relatives of many of your riders will be saved.

35. Assume this responsibility with all of the dedication and commitment as if you were being installed as the chairman of the deacons.

36. Always remember that this is a spiritual ministry and that many people will be in Heaven because of your bus ministry.

CHAPTER 29
THE SUNDAY SCHOOL DIRECTOR

1. Plan for an increased attendance of about 40 persons for each bus route established. Most of this increase will be in grades 1-6, as a rule. The largest increase will probably be in the third grade. Think in terms of 50% of the riders in grades 1-6, 20% preschool, 20% junior and senior high, and 10% adults. Of course this ratio will vary greatly in different areas but at least it gives some idea how to plan.

2. Remember that many churches have seen dramatic increases in attendances within a few weeks after launching a successful C.B.E. ministry. Many churches have doubled and tripled their average attendance within a few weeks. And most of this growth is in the Children's Division. So please be prepared. Start NOW!

3. Add additional workers as appropriate. Some new workers should be added at least one month before the bus routes are launched. This enables the new workers to gain experience just prior to the influx of new people.

4. Plan to add additional workers about one month prior to launching additional bus routes.

5. One good plan is to provide an extra teacher for each existing teacher in the divisions where the greatest influx is expected.

6. Give very special consideration to recruiting and training an adequate number of new workers. Keep in mind that new units will be needed.

7. Prepare your workers for any necessary adjustments of classes and rooms. It may be necessary for small classes to move to the small rooms in order for the large classes to have the large rooms.

8. Oftentimes it is necessary to use some space in a temporary way, such as previously unused rooms and space, the auditorium, hallways, dining area, kitchen, office space, nearby

121

residences, fire hall, public school buildings, public halls or auditoriums and even the buses themselves.

9. Point out to the workers that most of these children are unchurched and will act like unchurched children until taught otherwise. Some of those brought in may be different than "our kind" of children.

10. Remind the teachers of their major responsibility and glorious opportunity of visiting in the homes of these new people. Oftentimes a door is opened to these new families for a very effective witness.

11. Urge the outreach leaders to put their best foot forward in seeing that the proper number of visits are made into all of the homes of these new people.

12. Unless careful attention is given to this matter then many of the teachers and outreach workers will slow down on their visitation when their classes begin to show substantial growth. And if they do slow down, they are missing a real opportunity of going into these homes. They are also failing in one of their major responsibilities. Special guidance should be given in advance to make sure the teachers and outreach leaders do not fail in this important matter.

13. Instruct the Sunday School workers to give all necessary guidance to the new children (especially the smaller ones) so that they go directly to their worship areas at the close of the Sunday School.

14. Order an adequate quantity of additional literature well in advance. Be prepared to order additional literature each month or so as the bus routes develop and as you obtain a better idea as to age groups coming on the buses.

15. Have an adequate supply of the forms for enrolling new people. Make whatever arrangements are necessary to insure that all new people are promptly enrolled with the proper necessary information on each person. This will require some special planning, special procedures, and additional help for the Sunday School Secretary.

16. This is one distinct advantage of the orientation class for

newcomers. All of the correct information can be obtained during this class on their first Sunday.

17. Plan an orientation class for all newcomers in the Sunday School. This is basically for children with very little or no experience in Sunday School. All newcomers should be in this class the first Sunday. Then after the first Sunday it may be wise for any children with a fairly adequate Sunday School background to go on to their regular class.

18. The orientation class should continue for one month to begin with. Later these classes may be extended so as to last for two or three months.

19. These classes provide an opportunity for special Bible guidance for the children so as to integrate them in the most successful manner into the regular Sunday School classes. It also enables the pastor and various persons on the church staff and leadership to be introduced to these children. It is also a time to acquaint the children with the physical aspects of significant portions of the buildings and grounds.

20. Consider grading these orientation classes if a large number of new children are being brought in on the buses.

21. Consider a schedule where four bus teams are each averaging five new riders each Sunday. This means about 80 new people each month. One class for grades 1-3 and another class for grades 4-6. Each class continues for three months. And new classes begin each month. The following schedule gives an idea for consideration.

22. Teacher A begins an orientation class the first Sunday in January for all newcomers in grades 1-3. Teacher B begins one for grades 4-6. All newcomers in January in these grades enter these classes. These classes continue through March. Then these same teachers begin the same cycle in April.

23. Teacher C begins an orientation class the first Sunday in February for all newcomers in grades 1-3. Teacher D begins one for grades 4-6. All newcomers in February in these grades enter these classes. These classes continue through April. Then these same teachers begin the same cycle in May.

24. Teacher E begins an orientation class the first Sunday in March for all newcomers in grades 1-3. Teacher F begins one for grades 4-6. All newcomers in March in these grades enter these classes. These classes continue through May. Then these same teachers begin the same cycle in June.

25. This schedule requires a minimum of six teachers and six classrooms. This special effort would prepare the children to integrate with the regular classes in a more meaningful way.

CHAPTER 30
THE MUSIC DIRECTOR

1. Select songs and choruses to be sung on the buses.

2. Become familiar with the wide range of good songs and choruses that are being used or could be used on the buses.

3. Obtain a supply of the songs and choruses that are printed in large letters. The children learn them easier if they are printed large enough to be seen by all on the bus.

4. Careful attention should be given to selecting music that the children will enjoy and profit by.

5. Build a large file of all good music for children that will be helpful and acceptable.

6. Mimeograph an adequate supply of the words in a wide selection of songs and choruses.

7. Conduct training sessions for the Teenage Crusaders. There should be at least two and preferable three or four of these training sessions in the first few months.

8. Teach them the words and music of the various songs to be used.

9. Train them in leading the music on the bus. Let them take turns in leading the other teenagers in these sessions. Help them to obtain as much proficiency as possible in leading the music.

10. Instruct them that they are to stand at all times when leading the music on the bus. "One on his feet is better than three in the seat."

11. Instruct them to seat the riders to the rear of the bus. Seating the children in the rear of the bus and filling toward the front helps prevent some problems.

12. They should begin the singing after 10 or 12 riders have boarded the bus.

13. Some teenagers like to use an instrument (accordian, guitar, etc.) on the bus. These can be very helpful.

CHAPTER 31

THE TEENAGE CRUSADER

1. Attend the training sessions led by the Minister of Music. He will teach you songs and choruses to use on the buses. You will also gain some experience in leading the singing.

2. Be on the lookout for some one that can play an instrument on the bus, such as guitar, accordion, etc.

3. Plan to attend the meeting of the bus workers at 8:45 Saturday. This is usually a breakfast meeting.

4. Plan to help in enlisting riders the first Saturday. And you will need to go visiting with your bus team on Saturdays as often as you can.

5. Find out which bus team you will be on.

6. Know who will be in charge of the program on your bus on Sunday. If you are the one to be in charge then plan the details of your program. Plan all the songs you will use.

7. Have some understanding of the procedure for getting all the children into the proper rooms on Sunday morning.

8. Be familiar with the procedures of loading the children after church.

9. Find out the time and place to meet your bus team on Sunday morning—and be on time!

CHAPTER 32
THE MARTHA CLUB PRESIDENT

1. Obtain the names and telephone numbers of all those who are willing to serve in the Martha Club.

2. Obtain an idea as to the number that will be at the breakfast on Saturday.

3. Divide your members into different groups. Then determine how you want these groups to rotate.

4. Make sure that those on the group who are to prepare and serve breakfast on the first Saturday understand their assignments and that they will be present.

5. Plan a good healthy working man's breakfast. Many of the bus workers will spend most of Saturday out visiting.

6. See that adequate quantities of food and supplies are purchased.

7. Be familiar with the various arrangements, procedures, supplies, and so forth in the kitchen and the dining area.

8. Have a definite understanding as to the time that breakfast is to be served on Saturday. This is usually at 8:45.

9. Determine the time for meeting on Saturday to begin cooking breakfast.

10. Make whatever arrangements that are necessary about a key to the church building.

11. You may need to call your workers on Friday for last minute details and as a final reminder of the time for Saturday.

12. Remember that you are the unsung heroes of a major effort to evangelize your area.

CHAPTER 33
THE LEADER OF THE GRADED CHURCH SERVICES

1. It is usually best to begin the G.C.S. (Graded Church Services) at least one month or more before beginning the buses.

2. This enables you and your worker to obtain some valuable experience with a smaller group of children who are already accustomed to attending church.

3. Go and observe the G.C.S. in other churches that are successfully engaged in them. It is usually wise to go observe from two to five other churches with this type of ministry.

4. Arrange for your key workers to go and observe the G.C.S. in other churches.

5. Find out all the various materials, books, and program helps that are available. There is a fairly wide variety of helps available.

6. Obtain an adequate quantity of supplies and materials.

7. Decide the best way to grade the G.C.S. One common procedure is to begin with two groups—one group for the pre-schoolers and another for the first six grades.

8. Determine the best space to use for each age group.

9. Plan to further grade your G.C.S. as more children are brought in on the buses.

10. You will soon need three groups. These could be: pre-schoolers, grades 1-3, and grades 4-6.

11. Then as more children are brought in you may need four groups. These could be: preschoolers, grades 1-2, grades 3-4, and grades 5-6.

12. Later you will need to divide the preschoolers into two groups. Also you will need to begin one G.C.S. for grades 7-9. And some churches also have a G.C.S. for the high schoolers.

13. It is usually best to refer to each group in the G.C.S. by their ages or grades, as Grades 1-3 Church Service; Preschoolers

Church Service; Senior High Church Service; Age 5 Church Service and so on. This may be better than such titles as Children's Church, Junior Church, Little Church, etc. because these titles are not too descriptive.

14. Obtain an understanding of the procedure for counseling the children who respond to the Gospel. Check with the person in charge of the counseling abut all pertinent details.

15. Find out about the arrangements for refreshments for the children. These are usually served between Sunday School and church.

16. Check with the Minister of Music to learn who will play the music and lead the singing.

17. Compile a list of all workers and potential workers. Indicate on the list: their telephone numbers, the age group they prefer to work with, and the activity they prefer to handle.

18. Meet with the leaders of each age group for planning the various details about their services.

19. Decide who will be the leader for each age group of the G.C.S.

20. Plan the details for the offering. Offering plates, who takes it up, where is the money turned in, when in the order of service will it be, what to say to the children about the offering, who will lead the offertory prayer, and so on.

21. Plan the details for the various activities for the G.C.S. on the normal weekly program schedule.

PART VII
SOME PROBLEMS AND OTHER THINGS

CHAPTER 34
HANDLING PASTORIAL PROBLEMS

When a church begins bus evangelism the pastor will find he has new problems on his hands. He will have to face them day by day, and will have to make some new arrangements with people in the scope of his association. He may have twice the number of counseling cases, and twice the number of marriages and funerals. The pastor will have some problems that will be blessings, and some problems that will be heartaches. But increased problems are sure to come when a church engages itself in bus evangelism.

PROBLEMS FROM OTHER PASTORS

One of the problems that is sure to come is from other pastors. Pastors of neighboring churches will begin to complain that you are running your buses on "their territory." Some pastors will welcome your evangelistic outreach, but many will resent it, and suggest that you let them minister to the people in their area. That's fine, if they will do it. But most of the time they are not doing the job. Jesus said, "Go ye into all the world and preach the gospel to every creature." I believe He literally meant the whole world. It is my responsibility to reach every person I possibly can, regardless of where they live. Don't get worried when other pastors tell you to "get out of their territory." You just go ahead and do what Jesus said to do.

When we first started running buses at Beth Haven Baptist Church, a church wrote a bulletin-type letter to all of the people in the area where our bus was running. The letter called our church a "renegade" church, and warned the people against riding our bus. Then they bought a bus with an outside loudspeaker. As we would go around the route picking up riders, they would follow right behind our bus, and blare out, "Parents, do not allow your children to ride the blue bus from Beth Haven. They are out of their territory, and are a maverick church. Do not trust your children to the people of Beth Haven Church." Finally they came to the place where they had so little respect for us, they engaged in some very dangerous moves, such as passing our bus at 30 miles an hour, while we're in the process of picking up children! It wasn't long until the people of the area could see who had the real Christian attitude and concern for them.

That church still runs their bus in that area, and they bring in some people, but not as many as our bus does. But what is more important, that church probably would never have bought a bus at all if we had not run our bus in that area. And hundreds upon hundreds of people would have gone on through life without hearing the gospel. Many other churches in Louisville would not have buses now if we had not begun sending our buses in all directions. Now, on Sunday morning in Louisville, you may get run over by a church bus! We were the first church to run a bus into the Hazlewood Housing Project. Now there are at least 8 buses going into that area.

Some pastors will call and ask you not to run your buses near their church, but to "give them a chance." I was visiting on a route one day and met a pastor whose church was nearby. He said, "We're a small church trying to do our best. Give us a chance to reach these people." That church had been in the heart of Louisville for almost 100 years, and was running less than 200 in Sunday school. And that pastor was upset with me because I was running a bus in that area. The strangest thing was that I led a man and his wife to the Lord who lived right next door to that church! That pastor had never gone into that home right next door to his church to open the Bible and tell them about Jesus. But here he was, asking us to "give him a chance."

Other churches will ask you to stay out of their area because they are your "sister church." Yet, when we ran buses into that area, we brought over 150 people on two buses. Many of them were saved, and some are now Sunday school teachers, or in the bus ministry, or serving in some other capacity. That "sister" church has since bought some buses, and are bringing many to their church, too. But it would not have happened if we had not begun to run our buses in that area. I think God is pleased to see 6 buses from different churches running in that area, instead of no buses, and no one concerned about those people. I think competition between churches is good, and results in more souls being saved.

COMPLAINTS FROM OWN CHURCH MEMBERS

The second problem the pastor must face is complaints from his own church members. Some members will complain that some of the children literally stink. Shortly after coming to Beth Haven in 1969, a Sunday school lady came to me and said, "Mr. Gentry, you are ruining our church with these dirty, smelly children. You are ruining our church!" Well, the Bible tells us to "be ready always to give an answer to everyone who ask a reason of the hope that is within you." All I could do was to ask that lady, "Ma'am, I wonder which stinks the worst in the sight of God, that child's body or your attitude!" She did not have much to say, and she was not singing "Jesus Loves Me" as she walked away! But it wasn't long until that lady began to fall in love with some of the stinky, smelly, rag-doll children that came to our church. She began to take them home with her for Sunday lunch. She gave them a bath. She bought them clothes and shoes. She is now one of the hardest workers in our church, especially in helping the more needy ones.

Some members will complain about the things being written on the bathroom walls, and other places. These children have never been in church, and do not know the difference between church buildings and the movie-house, or the gymnasium. They must be taught the difference, but you can expect unusual things until they do learn better. Someone will complain that the padding on the pews is being marked. From the middle of the auditorium to the rear, our pews look like they were ordered with tic-tac-toe on them, and lots of hearts and arrows with initials such as G.S. loves A.D. And they are marked with ball-point pen, and cannot be cleaned off. But I had much rather have someone sitting there marking on the pew, than not having anyone there at all. These are the people who need to be saved, so you know you are preaching to lost people. But many will be more concerned about the building than about lost souls, and will complain.

You can also expect people to complain about the kids being rowdy. They will complain that there is too much noise, too much movement, and not the "reverence" there used to be. But boys and girls who have never been taught do not know they are not supposed to talk in church. Instead of not bringing the children, make the effort to teach them. If one is a continual talker, have the ushers move him. Sit him between two regular church members. When that child is sitting with Mr. Smith on one side and Mrs. Smith on the other, he soon learns to sit quitely in church.

There will be some destruction of property. For instance, when we began bringing in unchurched bus riders, I suggested to the pastor that we remove the little rubber gaskets that are in the holes that hold the communion cups. The pastor decided against that, and so we left them there. Well, the kids found they could pry them out fairly easily with a pencil or stick, and now there are very few gaskets left in the communion cup holders!

Some people will complain that the church is too crowded. Some people would rather come to a small church than have a lot of people—especially children—in the services. As the crowds grow, you will need to begin Children's church serivces. You will need to put chairs in the aisles. The front of the church will be filled with people who respond to the invitation.

Some people will complain that the kids who ride the bus get special favors and treats, while the kids who come with their parents do not. In our church, all the children in the pre-school and first and second grades get Kool-Aid and cookies in their Sunday school classes every week. And some people will complain about this, too! Satan does not like full churches, souls saved, and people serving God. So when your church begins to move, you can expect friction as Satan begins to oppose.

Finances will be another source of problems. Some will say the church cannot afford a bus evangelism ministry. They will point out the difficulty the church is having in meeting the current bond program, the need for repairs to the roof, the need for additional equipment, etc. They will think of a hundred reasons why the church cannot afford a bus evangelism program. Yet church after church that could not afford it have launched successful bus evangelism programs, and God supplies their needs. We need to depend on God's provision, not on what we can see.

PEOPLE ASKING FOR HELP

Then, you can expect calls from people asking for help. People will ask for food, clothing, furniture, legal help, medical help and cash money. You cannot possibly meet all the needs that will come, but you can try to find some in your congregation, or in your community who will donate some service, goods or money to help these people.

BAPTISMS: A PROBLEM

Believe it or not, baptisms will become a problem. It will be a problem because you will need to baptize every Sunday morning, and maybe even every Sunday night, too. At Beth Haven we baptize three times each week, and during revivals, we baptize every night! You will need to prepare to baptize by setting up small cubicles where the candidates can change their clothes in privacy. All people, even boys and girls, want privacy when they take off their clothes, especially if strangers are in the same areas. Be sure to have enough towels and baptisimal clothing. We bought pants and white shirts for the boys and men to wear. If you do this, you will find it a great advantage to split the trouser legs from the cuff to the knee. They are much easier to get off that way. For the girls and women we bought heavy white bleached muslin. That material soaks up the water quickly, and will not float upward in the water. This prevents any embarrassment or immodesty. We also provide underwear and bobby sox for them. We provide all different sizes of clothings, so that when a candidate comes, the lady in the dressing room area can direct each person to a booth containing the appropriate size of clothing. It takes about three to four minutes for a candidate to be directed to the changing booth to the time they are ready to be baptized. In the same way, it takes our pastor about one minute from the time he leaves the pulpit to the time he is in the baptisimal pool wearing his waders and baptisimal jacket. Our people do not grow restless waiting for the baptisms to begin. And they know it will be about one minute from the time the last person is baptized to the time the pastor will again be behind the pulpit to dismiss the congregation.

These are some of the problems that will come. But with proper leadership all problems can be worked out to the glory of God. Everything rises or falls on leadership, so be a good leader. Plan ahead, plan efficiently, and then do it!

CHAPTER 35
BUSES THAT DID NOT RUN

(the following is the content of a Saturday morning bus pastor's meeting held at Beth Haven Baptist Church)

A lot of churches want the bus ministry, but they won't do anything about it. They won't survey the situation, they won't speak out to get the help, they won't come and visit other churches to find out how to go about it.

Then there are those who say they want it, but think they can't afford it. They say, "We'd like to have a bus ministry, but we just can't afford one. We're a small church, and our budget just won't allow us to have a bus. We want it, but we just can't afford it."

There are some churches that have a bus ministry, but don't really want it! There was a church just north of Akron, Ohio, that had 12 buses. One day they gave the bus director an ultimatum. They said if the buses did not do so much by a certain date, they were going to sell them!" God help a pastor who says he's going to get rid of the bus ministry. You know what that tells me? That tells me that rascal was just too lazy to get out and visit! It also tells me that he was too lazy to inspire others to do the job. It tells me that he was listening to all the whims and complaints of the people in the church. Instead of listening to God, and getting the job done, he's been listening to the people, and falling down on the job!

There are churches that don't want the bus ministry. They are the ones who say, "We don't want those smelly people." "We don't want our church filled up." "We can't minister to those kind of people." Listen, if you can't minister to people like that, then you'd better cancel your trip to heaven, because it's going to be mighty crowded up there with "people like that!" I wonder what they would have said on the day of Pentecost. "Oh, there's too many people coming forward. You'd better stop some of those. We don't want that many to get saved today. Let's scatter them out over three or four years time. Let's kind of figure this out, and set up a schedule by which they can get saved. There's no sense trying to get them saved since we don't have any place to put them."

INDIFFERENT CHURCHES

No, God said to do it now. These are some of the reasons a bus does not run. Because of indifferent churches, or churches that are ignorant of what is going on in the bus ministry, or churches that are more concerned about their seating capacity, than they are about souls going to Hell!

LOVE THE WORLD MORE

Now here's another reason that buses do not run. It's because of bus pastors that love the world more than they love God. God help you men if you ever get to the place where you think the cares of this world are more pressing upon you than the cares for God's work. Now, there's probably one or two bus workers still laying back in bed. Well, I'm going to pray just like the pastor did in the last church I was in. He told his people on Sunday night, "If you're not here for the bus meeting on Monday and Tuesday, I'm going to pray that God will give you boils on your butt, and you won't be able to sit down for six months!" He stood right up there in the church, a big, beautiful church—carpeted throughout, stained glass windows, and everything—and said he was going to pray that God would put boils on their you-know-what! And we had a good turnout for the meeting! Some 30 people came forward at the invitation to get into the bus ministry. Some were professional people, some were everyday workers, some had a good education, some were students, some were uneducated.

I don't want God to have to deal with you too harshly. I hope that God just burdens your heart, and you'll judge yourself. The Bible says that if you will judge yourself, He will not judge you. So judge yourself. But pastors that love the world too much, they are the ones who cause buses not to run. If you love the world too much, your bus will not run. Dr. Roberson gave some excuses in a sermon entitled, "Why?" A little girl, he said, had called him one Sunday night. The little girl said, "Dr. Roberson, the bus hasn't come by to pick me up. Is the bus going to come and get us? We've been waiting for the bus

to come on Sunday night. Why doesn't it come?" Does that
strike a chord with you? I wonder if there's anyone out there
on Sunday nights that wants to come on your bus? Do you come
to church on Sunday night wondering if some of your people
would like to come? A lot of buses don't run on Sunday night.
Why? Because we say we don't have time, or we are too tired,
or it would just take too much time. I can just see that little
girl standing on the porch—probably with her little Bible in her
hand—out there waiting for the bus to come. I guess she waited
for about 30 minutes after it should have come, and then she
began to worry. Maybe the bus was broken down—or maybe
the bus pastor was indifferent, and just didn't care if the bus
ran or not.

WRONG MOTIVE

Another reason that a lot of buses don't run is because people
have the wrong motive for things. They want to bring glory to
themselves, and to their church. After a while, God just cuts
them off, and that's it. And they begin to struggle. I'll never
forget what my pastor said. He said the perfect will of God
comes easy. When we're in the perfect will of God, things
come easy for us. But when we're in the acceptable will of God,
it's work, work, work, work. You just beat your head off. It's
just like being fenced in. Everything turns to sour grapes. It's
just like everything else you try to do—nothing works right,
everything breaks down. The main reason for that is because we
don't pray enough! Does anyone disagree with that? Do you
think you pray too much? Have you prayed for the pastor this
week? Have you prayed for me this week? Have you prayed
for lost souls to be saved this week? Have you prayed for the
financial needs of your church this week? Have you prayed
for the deacons this week? Have you prayed that God will
make them unusual men, and that we'd have an unusual church?

We're real prayer warriors, aren't we? What do we pray for?
"Oh, Lord, look our electricity is going to be cut off. Lord,
would you help us get the electric bill paid? And Lord, little
Susie's sick. I want you to help her." Yes, we pray for all these
things that we want, but how about God's work? The Bible
says you have not because you ask not. Is that right? The Bible

says, as a man thinketh, so is he. A man starts thinking about wanting great deacons, wanting a great bus route, wanting great things done for God. He begins to pray about it. A lot of times we have the wrong motive. Too often we just want to bring glory to self, but I'm sure our men are not that way. Our men have been preached to enough in the bus pastors meeting, and on Sunday night, and at other times to know that if we do it for self, we'll fall on our face!

SATAN HINDERS US

Another reason is because Satan hinders us. Self will hinder you, but I think that Satan laughs at buses that don't run. And I think that if Satan had a car, and could ride up Johnsontown Road, and look over that parking lot on Sunday morning, and see the buses that do not run, he would laugh. Whenever we give an invitation, and ask for bus pastors to come down the aisle and no one comes, I think old Satan laughs. But you know, we could stop a lot of his laughter, if we prayed about it. If we'd really get earnest with God about the thing, I think that a lot of buses don't because there isn't a program on the bus. There's no program on the bus because we haven't prayed about it, . . . and old Satan laughs. Now I've said it time and time again—there are three things that make a bus ministry go. I've analyzed it, and I'm convinced that there are three things that make your bus route go. Without these three things, you might as well fold up your suitcase and leave town. Number one is a plea to the parent. If you're not begging that parent to let the child come, then you're not going to get them. You can get all the kids you want excited about coming, but when that kid goes in the house and tells his Mama, "I want to go to church tomorrow" that doesn't ring a bell with her. You've got to see that parent and make the appeal right there. Number two is a good program on the bus. And number three is your own prayer life. Without these three things, you can't have it. If I were to measure our bus ministry against bus ministries across the nation, I'd measure it by what goes on here on Saturday night. I haven't been to one church yet that came up and told me about their great prayer meeting. And it's not just the Saturday night prayer meeting, but the prayer

meetings that go on every night of the week here. You know a
church is going somewhere when it gets on its knees! But when
you try to go without prayer, you're not going to go too far.
You will go as far as the flesh can take you, and then you're
going to fall. A lot of buses don't run because Satan is laughing
at them. But he doesn't laugh when a bus does run.

We're praying that God will give us 25 more bus pastors
by this time next year. Then we'll be running 50 buses instead
of 22. Then we are asking God for 75 by the end of 1973, and
100 by December 1974! Now listen, there are some reasons
why a bus doesn't run. Why isn't your bus running? I've been
writing down almost everything the pastor says when he
preaches, but last Sunday night, some of the things he said
got to me. He mentioned, "What do you want most in life?
Things, glory, position, security? What do you want most?" I'd
say that every bus pastor in this room wants a full bus load.
But do you know why he wants it? It's because he wants to see
people saved! Then the pastor said, "What do you think about
most?" What's on your mind, Don? The place up there where
you work? The bus ministry? Going to some other church? Just
what is on your mind most? A lot of teenagers will think of a
boy friend, or girl friend. And we think about our family, and
we think about our job. But what do you think of most?

Then he said, "What do you use your money for most?" How
about that one? Are you giving God what belongs to Him? I
sure hope you do. But the thing he said that got to me the most

HOW YOU USE YOUR LEISURE TIME

was, "What do you do with most of your leisure time?" Well,
let me ask you, when do you have leisure time? It's sure not on
Saturday or Sunday! Monday nights seems to be about it. And
that's after you come home from working all day. Slick, what
do you do with most of your leisure time? Run souls for the
Lord? Yes, you go out and get people. And you run about 200
on your bus route each week. There's a fellow that doesn't have
too much time for leisure. Mike, what do you do besides making
visits on your leisure time? Nothing much? Not a man in this
room has too much leisure time. You men don't have any
leisure time!

Someone asked what you do for recreation, and one bus pastor said his recreation was seeing the bus full on Sunday! That's my greatest joy, too—seeing the buses filled on Sunday. Now lots of folks have time to cook a barbecue, mow the lawn, fix the car, plan a vacation—but not the men here. They don't plan a vacation unless they can come back and visit their bus route on Saturday. Oh, we've got a few that will go off and leave their route unvisited, but I don't think they are going to do it next year. You wouldn't do that, would you Mike? How far did you come back to visit your route this year? He just came back from Florida. He got down there on the beach, and got to thinking about his route, and got convicted. So he got up and came back to visit his bus route on Saturday and Sunday. We need some more men like that. Slick Goodman said he'd never plan another vacation on a weekend. Now that's when you get down to doing God's business. That's what makes this bus ministry here different from other places.

WHERE YOU SPEND YOUR TIME

Then the pastor said, "Who would you rather spend your time with?" Bob, who would you rather spend your time with? Oh, the people of the church, and on your bus route. How about you, Al, where would you like to spend most of your time? Where would you rather spend most of your time, Vic? Now listen, I'm getting down to this. Who do you want to spend your time with? If you want to spend it with God, then you're spiritual. If you want to spend it with the world, then you're unspiritual. Now, you say, "Oh, but I love God." No you don't, either! When you love your girl-friend, you'll go see her. And when you love God's work, you'll go and do it!

WHO YOU ADMIRE MOST

Then the pastor said, "Who do you admire most?" Some teenagers say, "The Monkees." Others say "The Beetles." Some say this, and some say that. Who would you say that you admired most, Bernie? I know you admire the Lord more than your wife, because the Lord has never whipped you like she has! A lot of men admire sports figures, like Joe Namath, or Johnny Unitas. Here in Kentucky, many men admire the basket-

ball greats that we have. Well, fellows, if you really admire the
Lord Jesus the most, you'll have more from Him. But if you've
got to take your Saturday afternoons to watch the Colts play,
or someone else, then your mind is not really on the Lord! Now
it's great to have some kind of recreation time. Glenn, you're
not married, and you've got to have some kind of recreation.
I know you've got to have some at some time, but do it after
you retire. Wait until you get 75, and then relax!

WHAT DO YOU LAUGH AT?

Then the pastor asked, "What do you laugh at most?" You
know what tickles me most? There's two or three times I've
got real tickled at Don Choate. When we had the September
push on, he came in one morning, and I told him some church
in California wanted him. He didn't even tell me how many
came on his bus that morning. He jumped about two feet high,
and ran off to find his wife and tell her about it. He was laughing and talking so much, he didn't even help his people off the
bus. But then I've seen Don come in with 14 or 15, and one
time I remember he had 12 on his bus. He got off his bus, and
went over to the side of his car. I thought he was going to move
it. I didn't know what he was doing, but he sure didn't want
to say anything to anybody. I had to laugh about that. "Don's
really down in the dumps," I thought. And he thinks I'm really
going to get him. When I did see him, I chewed him, alright,
but I was laughing on the inside. I was trying to help him up,
and now he's doing a lot better. Last month Don averaged
83 per Sunday. That's pretty good for a fellow who can't talk
too good when he gets up to the door. But once he gets going,
you can't get him stopped! If he had someone to visit with
him, I think he'd stay out there every day of the week. He loves
the bus ministry. And there's a lot of things that he's laughed at.
And a lot of things we all have laughed at. If you could see
some of the things that go on around here, and some of the kids
on the buses, you'd about die laughing. Little Phillip, on one
of the routes, tickles me every time I see him. And how about
Everett? See, just mention Everett, and many of you start to
laugh. What makes you laugh the most? Is it the Lord, and
the Lord's work? Or is it some old dirty jokester on TV? Where

is your laughter coming from? Is it from a spiritual source? From something you're trying to do, and you've had some fun doing? What causes a bus not to run? Your leisure time spent the wrong way? The person you admire most—is that stopping your bus route? These are some things I have found that cause a bus not to run. I want our buses to run. Last week I think there were about 35 people saved, and about 15 baptized. That was really a bad Sunday for us. We usually baptize 25 or 30 a week, and have about 50 saved. But I'm praying that God will help us, and that our buses will never stop running. I pray that God will use you men to do what God wants you to do today. There are some people here to visit with you, and I know we will all want to visit. We've got things to do, and I hope that we don't have any "honeydews" that will have to go back home. There is nothing more important than God's work, and there are some men here today who have come to learn from you because you are an example. You are the fruit tree they have come to pick off of, because God has planted you, and made you a tall tree in God's service. These men have come to glean from you today. Don't say that you are too tired today, or that you have something else that must be done today. Don't say you can't take one of these visitors with you today. If you do, then somebody's bus won't run. What causes buses not to run? Maybe the fact that sometimes we don't care as we ought. I go week after week, to church after church. When I first started doing this, it was a great thing. But after a while, you become tired, and you say, "Oh, if only I had stayed home!" I told the pastor that one day, and he just reminded me that after I die, they can lay me to rest. Then I can rest, and rest, and rest all I want to. But just as sure as I died and was buried, the rapture would take place the next day, and I wouldn't get to rest at all! But I want to go on for the Lord. I want to go on, and on, and on for Him. I want to be sure that somewhere the buses are going to run. I want to be sure that new buses are going to run. I want to be sure that more buses are going to run, and will keep on running for Jesus!

CHAPTER 36
LOST RIDERS

We are not talking now about being spiritually lost, but physically lost. One day a little girl will ride your bus to Sunday school and church. But, on the way home, when you stop at her door, you discover she is not on your bus! Brother, that will make cold chills run all over you, even on a hot day! And then you have to go tell the parents that their child is not on your bus, and you don't know exactly where she is. The parents may become frantic. Once, the parents wanted to call the police down on us! But if this happens, be sure to do all you can to keep them calmed down until the child is found. Better yet, here some tips to keep this from happening: 1. Mark every hand as the kids get on the bus with the same number as the route number. Do this with a ball-point pen or a felt marker. Most stamp-pad marks will come off on a hot day, so don't depend on them. If every hand is marked, all the bus pastor need do is check every one as they get back on the bus. That way, it is impossible for a child to get on the wrong bus. Of all cases of lost children, 99% are the result of children getting on the wrong bus. The rest usually result from the child deciding to walk home from church without telling the parents or the bus pastor.

2. In talking with the parent, assume that the child got on the wrong bus. Explain to them that as soon as one of the bus pastors realizes he has a child with a number that does not match his route, he will bring the child directly home. Assure them that their child will be home in 1½ hours or less. Usually the parents will understand. And they don't have a hard time accepting the fact that their child simply got on the wrong bus.

3. The hardest one to solve is when one child decides to go home with another, and gets on and off the wrong bus unnoticed. All the buses come back, and no one has any kids left over! You must then call the parents and ask them to call the homes of their child's best friends. Usually the lost child is found after 2 or 3 calls. But you can be sure that a bus pastor needs only one experience like this, and he will be very sure that he has all his little lambs every Sunday.

CHAPTER 37

BETH HAVEN BAPTIST CHURCH
5515 Johnsontown Road
Louisville, Kentucky 40272

Dear Tremendous Bus Driver:
I want to thank you for the important job you are doing for the Lord in driving God's bus on Sundays—without you we could not operate that route in an efficient manner. You are now chauffering for the King of the Universe—our Lord Jesus Christ. He is the co-pilot on every bus.

I want to ask a big favor of you. Would you help me and your Bus Pastor in keeping the bus clean? I belive if we can once get them clean we will be able to keep them that way. I would like for you to be in charge of this—use your teenage helper to help you. I will see to it that your bus has a broom and dust cloth on it, perhaps you can keep a cardboard box in the front for litter. This will help a lot.

If you would like to take the bus home for a day or two to get it in good shape, this would be all right with me. I ask your help in any possible way to keep this bus clean.

Let me mention some safety rules that must be obeyed:

1. Please stop at all rail road crossings, regardless of whether loaded or empty. Three children were killed on a church bus in Fort Wayne, Indiana because the driver did not stop.
2. No bus is to be driven above the speed limit, or above 55 miles per hour at any time.
3. If you hear a buzzing sound, it means that the back door is open.
4. No smoking is ever allowed on the church bus. It is a bad testimony to those on and off the bus.
5. Never leave the bus motor running without an ADULT in the driver's seat.

145

6. When you park, always set the emergency brake, and remove the keys from the switch.
7. Never back a bus without some one guiding you from outside the bus.
8. Be aware that some people will pull up close to your back bumper, so if you roll back your bus will hit them and they will sue the church.
9. Check your turn signals and lights each time you drive.
10. Help us save God's buses by watching those indicators, *OIL* and *WATER*. When the oil pressure drops or the bus heats up, please pull the bus aside *right then* and call for assistance. Don't try to limp in to the church. That may be all it takes to ruin that engine.
11. It is unlawful to operate the bus with the door open.

> Your friend in Christ,
> Gardiner Gentry
> Bus Ministry Director

CHAPTER 38
WORKERS REQUEST SHEET

After much prayer and consideration, I feel it is God's will that I serve in one or more of the following places:

Bus Pastor_____
Mainly responsible to see that the bus is filled every Sunday morning.

Associate Bus Pastor_____
Will be responsible *one* weekend per month for duties of Bus Pastor.

Bus Driver_____
Will see that bus is ready to roll Sunday Morning, excluding major maintenance, but including gas and cleanliness of inside.

Assistant Bus Driver_____
Will be responsible one weekend per month for duties of Bus Driver, and subject to emergency call.

Helpers_____
Ride the bus and see to safety and comfort of passengers; lead singing.

Mechanics_____
Work and assist Maintenance Director in keeping buses rolling.

Canvasser_____
Work one Saturday per month to saturate a new area to either start a new area or add to an old one.

Breakfast Chef (Martha Club)_____
Be responsible for preparing breakfast on Saturday mornings for bus teams for *one month.* I prefer the month of

Sanders, tapers and painters_____

> To be present to help sand the bus bodies, tape the windows, and/or paint the inside and/or outside.

Prayer_____

> To pray daily for the success of the Bus Ministry—Not for the glory of any one individual or any group of individuals or even for Beth Haven Baptist Church, but to the glory of our Lord and Savior, Jesus Christ.

Name _____

Address _____

Telephone _____

CHAPTER 39

SOME KEY VERSES FROM THE BUS WORKERS' TRANSLATION OF THE BIBLE

1. "And behold, the hour surely cometh—the hour of the great departure—when some children will attempt to board the chariot without the chariot number written on their hands, only to hear the Pastor say, 'Depart from me, I never knew you'! And there shall be weeping and patter of feet as they begin the long walk home." Chevrolet 19:20

2. "Therefore, to the horseman who knoweth how to drive a chariot safely, and doeth it not—for him, the insurance premiums shall surely be increased." Superior 4:12

3. "Beware of the false prophets—and legion is their name—who glory in revealing the good reasons why the Bus Pastor cannot go out visiting his bus route Saturday. Forget thou not, my son, these are prophets of lesser gods. Have no fellowship with them for they shall soon fade away." Dodge 6:10

4. "Be not deceived, the Bus Director is not fooled, when the sleepy Bus Pastor blameth his tardiness on the slow driving habits of his leading horseman as he rolleth his chariot up the ramp at 9:50." Alarm Clock 6:15

5. "Sad is that unforgetable day when the horseman faileth to feed the horse and the horse quiteth running as he picketh up the lambs. For only the rejoicing of the lambs during the wait for them to bring some hay from the stable can soothe his seered conscious for depending upon the stable boy to feed his horse the day before." Gas tank 1:1

6. "The evil one prepareth a special place for the Bus Pastor who picketh up little lambs who standeth waiting for another chariot to take them to another pasture." Unscrupulous 13:13

7. "Woe unto that person who stealeth precious gasoline out of

the chariots for his fuel system shall surely be burst as-
sunder." Ford 2:15

8. "Blessed is that teenage couple who falleth in love while
   taking the children back home—for their ride back to the
   church is sweeter than honey out of the beehive." Cupid 3:16

9. "Woe unto that driver who backeth his chariot without the
   benefit of outside guidance, because he cometh, much
   quicker than he thinketh, to a sudden and shattering stop."
   Transmission 3:23

10. "Go ye therefore, unless you are too busy in other things,
    and teach everyone, within one mile of your church build-
    ing, if they seem to be in a receptive mood, and then baptize
    them, if their parents will permit it, in any manner they pre-
    fer, at any convenient time after they have proven them-
    selves throughout the waiting period, and then teach them
    all theology and church doctrine, if they will attend church
    every Sunday night, remember to call me if you need help
    and my line is not busy." Bluebird 28:19-20

11. "For there hath no temptation taken the Bus Pastor to omit
    Saturday's route visitation but such as is common to all other
    Bus Pastors—and much to be rewarded is the Pastor who
    overcometh these temptations." I Hobby 2:12

12. "Behold, my heart asketh as I looketh on my left hand and
    as I looketh on my right hand and I beholdeth my kinsmen
    who cometh by every Saturday and Sunday because they
    careth for the souls of my little ones. Me thinks perhaps I
    goeth soon to their church and seeth why they careth so
    much for my little ones. Perhaps they leadeth me soon be-
    side the still waters also." Adult 23:5

13. "Pray ye, therefore, for special strength on that inevitable
    Monday evening when the pious prophet from status quo
    church riseth to his feet at the Pastor's Conference and in-
    quireth the attitude of the clergy toward the shepherd who
    invadeth the vineyards of others with his chariots loaded
    with bubblegum and transporteth the little lambs to far
    away lands." II Gear 4:16

14. "Wisdom faileth, bedlam exists, and folly reigneth, on high
    attendance Sunday when the Sunday School Director

learneth he cannot put two gallons of honey in a one gallon bucket—notwithstanding the fact that he prayeth earnestly about it the week before." Overcrowded 48:96

15. "Blessed indeed is the horseman that winneth first prize in the contest for the cleanest and sharpest chariot." Faithful 15:58

16. "The day cometh—and even now approacheth much faster than thou thinkest—when the church chariots create traffic jams each Sunday morning as they picketh up little lambs, and taketh them to the various grazing pastures." Good News 3:16

17. "Beware of the child which concealeth a toy weapon—lest the loaded chariot bound for Sunday School be hi-jacked to the nearest amusement park instead." Recreation 3:3

18. "How eternally grateful is the horseman with a weak generator on his chariot, for the worker who findeth the jumper cables on a cold winter morning." Delay 5:17

19. "Blessed is the Bus Pastor who tieth the shoe and combeth the hair of the little lamb while the mother sleepeth and the driver bloweth the horn—for he shall surely receive two extra points in the contest." I Runnerup 2:8

BUS DIRECTORS SCHOOL
BETH HAVEN BAPTIST CHURCH

5515 Johnsontown Road
LOUISVILLE, KENTUCKY 40272

Director
Rev. Gardiner Gentry

CURRICULUM
INCLUDES

Building
Your
Bus Ministry

Bus
Mechanics

Motivation

Promotion

Children's
Church

BIBLE

Sunday
School

WORDS FROM BROTHER GARDINER............

The Bus Director's School at Beth Haven is going great! God gave twenty-four choice men for the first semester. Many of these men have already built great bus routes to over 100; some over 150. Others are being used in the Children's Church, others excelling in the field of Soul Winning. One student from North Carolina had never won a soul, he now wins as high as 5 or more per week.

Classes are at night from 6:30 p.m. until 9:30 p.m. This gives the students a chance to work in most any field. Some work in construction, banking, teaching, food stores, hospitals, etc.

Many new students will be coming in January for the beginning of the second semester. God's hand is upon the Director's School.

1. Because there is a great need for this field of work in the ministry.

2. Because pastors call here, and ask for trained men, who know how to set up and work a Bus Ministry, Visitation Program, and Children's Church Ministry.

3. Because this is a one year program, designed to get a man on the field with a specialized ministry.

4. Because this school gives training beyond the class room.

A student was overheard making this statement: "I believe this school was started just for me." He was a top quality bus pastor in his church, but felt the call of God to full-time service in the field of Bus Ministry, Outreach, and Children's Church.

God is looking for men to use in the field of Bus Evangelism. If He is calling you, remember, this school could have been started just for you.

Bring Them In

FOR CHURCH GROWTH THROUGH BUS EVANGELISM

JUST A PERSONAL WORD

from the desk of
S. RAY SADLER

BRING THEM IN MAGAZINE has one clearly stated objective—A PROGRAM OF SATURATION EVANGELISM FOR EVERY CITY IN AMERICA! ! Great masses of our people all over this land are shackled by the blinding, binding power of Satan. The staff of this magazine has one purpose—to see them freed by the power of the gospel of Jesus Christ. We believe that the *Local Church* must be the carrier of this good news—and thus we are dedicated to sharing the methods used by people who are doing that job. Our writers, in the past and in the future, come from a cross-section of the best in their fields in the country. Our only requirement is that they preach Jesus crucified and resurrected and that they be successful in the field about which they write.

Our philosophy is one thing—building great churches and reaching great masses of people to the glory of Christ! ! The stories we are reporting and the articles we are sharing are success stories written by successful people.

Personally, I am tired of teachers that don't teach, preachers that don't preach, leaders that don't lead, and writers that do not know what they are writing about.

No group or denomination has a corner on the gospel, or God's people. BRING THEM IN is designed to promote local church evangelism, rather than a particular denominational point of view. It is for all who really want to reach people for Christ now! We welcome contributions from all who have a success story to tell, or something that will help and encourage others to do a better job.

I am not an ecumaniac—but I do believe that the hour is late and that we who preach the Book, the Blood, and the Blessed Hope have a vast responsibility to win as many to Christ as is possible! Let's join hands and hearts and share Christ with America! ! It must be done, it will be done, and it can be done! !

CONTRIBUTING EDITORS

Rev. Gardiner Gentry
Beth Haven Baptist Church
Louisville, Kentucky

Mr. Leonard Hinton
Park Avenue Baptist Church
Nashville, Tennessee

Rev. Larry Lewis
Baptist Convention of
Pennsylvania-South Jersey
Harrisburg, Pennsylvania

Mrs. Rubye G. Pate
Sanders Manufacturing Company
Nashville, Tennessee

Rev. William A. Powell
Home Mission Board
Southern Baptist Convention
Atlanta, Georgia

SUBSCRIPTION INFORMATION

1 yr.—$2.00; 2 yrs.—$3.50;
3 yrs.—$5.00

Have you a story to tell? A blessing to share? Some comment or criticism on what you read in *"BRING THEM IN?"* As well as being informative and inspirational, *"BRING THEM IN"* constitutes a forum for an exchange of ideas.

BRING THE IN
Let me tell you how pleased I am with the magazine "Bring Them In." Many helpful suggestions have been gleaned from its pages as well as it being a source of encouragement for our bus pastors.

> Pastor, Randall M. Jones
> Hillcrest Baptist Church
> Greer, South Carolina

Dear BTI,
I just finished reading the May, 1972 issue of *BRING THEM IN,* and it was a tremendous blessing to my heart.
Thank you for the magazine, and keep up the motivation that we need to win the world for Christ.

> S. S.
> Stillwater, Okla.

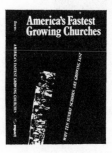